DATE DUE

MAR 1 5	2010		
NOV 2 9	2012		

Demco, Inc. 38-293

Assisted Suicide

Lauri S. Friedman

Current Issues

ReferencePoint Press™

San Diego, CA

About the Author

Lauri S. Friedman earned her bachelor's degree in religion and political science from Vassar College in 1999. Her studies there focused on political Islam, and she produced a thesis on the Islamic Revolution in Iran titled *Neither West, Nor East, but Islam.* She also holds a preparatory degree in flute performance from the Manhattan School of Music.

Friedman is the founder of LSF Editorial, a writing and editing outfit in San Diego. Her clients include ReferencePoint Press, for whom she has written *The Death Penalty, Nuclear Weapons and Security, Terrorist Attacks, Abortion,* and Islam, all in the Compact Research series.

Friedman lives in Ocean Beach, San Diego, with her husband, Randy, and their yellow lab, Trucker. In her spare time she enjoys spending time with family and friends, cooking, making music, taking Trucker to the beach, traveling, and planning her next writing project.

Picture credits:
Maury Aaseng: 32–35, 51–52, 54, 70–73, 88–91
AP Images: 15
Photoshot: 12

LIBRARY OF CONGRESS CATALOGING-IN-PUBLICATION DATA

Friedman, Lauri S.
  Assisted suicide / by Lauri S. Friedman.
    p. cm. — (Compact research)
  Includes bibliographical references and index.
  ISBN-13: 978-1-60152-048-7 (hardback)
  ISBN-10: 1-60152-048-4 (hardback)
  1. Assisted suicide—Popular works. I. Title.
  R726.F725 2008
  179.7—dc22

                                                    2008039089

Contents

Foreword

"Where is the knowledge we have lost in information?"

—T.S. Eliot, "The Rock."

As modern civilization continues to evolve, its ability to create, store, distribute, and access information expands exponentially. The explosion of information from all media continues to increase at a phenomenal rate. By 2020 some experts predict the worldwide information base will double every 73 days. While access to diverse sources of information and perspectives is paramount to any democratic society, information alone cannot help people gain knowledge and understanding. Information must be organized and presented clearly and succinctly in order to be understood. The challenge in the digital age becomes not the creation of information, but how best to sort, organize, enhance, and present information.

ReferencePoint Press developed the *Compact Research* series with this challenge of the information age in mind. More than any other subject area today, researching current issues can yield vast, diverse, and unqualified information that can be intimidating and overwhelming for even the most advanced and motivated researcher. The *Compact Research* series offers a compact, relevant, intelligent, and conveniently organized collection of information covering a variety of current topics ranging from illegal immigration and methamphetamine to diseases such as anorexia and meningitis.

The series focuses on three types of information: objective single-author narratives, opinion-based primary source quotations, and facts and statistics. The clearly written objective narratives provide context and reliable background information. Primary source quotes are carefully selected and cited, exposing the reader to differing points of view. And facts and statistics sections aid the reader in evaluating perspectives. Presenting these key types of information creates a richer, more balanced learning experience.

For better understanding and convenience, the series enhances information by organizing it into narrower topics and adding design features that make it easy for a reader to identify desired content. For example, in *Compact Research: Illegal Immigration*, a chapter covering the economic impact of illegal immigration has an objective narrative explaining the various ways the economy is impacted, a balanced section of numerous primary source quotes on the topic, followed by facts and full-color illustrations to encourage evaluation of contrasting perspectives.

The ancient Roman philosopher Lucius Annaeus Seneca wrote, "It is quality rather than quantity that matters." More than just a collection of content, the *Compact Research* series is simply committed to creating, finding, organizing, and presenting the most relevant and appropriate amount of information on a current topic in a user-friendly style that invites, intrigues, and fosters understanding.

Assisted Suicide at a Glance

Legalized Assisted Suicide
Physician-assisted (PAS) suicide is explicitly legal in just four places in the world—Oregon, Washington, the Netherlands, and Switzerland.

Prohibited Assisted Suicide Around the World
Physician-assisted suicide is explicitly illegal in Canada, Hungary, Italy, New Zealand, Norway, Russia, and the United Kingdom.

Prohibited Assisted Suicide in the United States
Physician-assisted suicide is explicitly illegal in seven states—Iowa, Louisiana, Maryland, Michigan, Rhode Island, South Carolina, and Virginia. Many others have defeated ballot initiatives that proposed to legalize the practice.

Number of Assisted Suicides in Oregon
Since 1997, 341 people have used Oregon's Death with Dignity Act to die.

Assisted Suicide Rate
Less than 1 percent of all deaths in Oregon—about 0.15 percent—occur as a result of physician-assisted suicide. The rate is about the same in Switzerland—0.2 percent—and in the Netherlands—0.1 percent.

Age of Those Who Use Assisted Suicide
The median age of people who have elected assisted suicide in Oregon is 69.

Race of Those Who Use Assisted Suicide
In Oregon 97.4 percent of people who have died by assisted suicide have been white.

Education Level of Those Who Use Assisted Suicide

Oregonians with a bachelor's degree or higher are 7.9 times more likely to elect physician-assisted suicide than those without a high school diploma.

Diseases of Those Who Use Assisted Suicide

More than 80 percent of people who elect physician-assisted suicide in Oregon are suffering from some form of cancer.

Potential for Abuse

A 2007 study published in the *Journal of Medical Ethics* examined 10 vulnerable groups—including the poor, the disabled, minorities, and the young—and found that none showed any sign of being threatened by legalized assisted suicide.

Assisted Suicide and Depression

Only about 5 percent of patients who elect physician-assisted suicide in Oregon undergo a mental health consultation to determine if they are depressed.

Why People Elect Physician-Assisted Suicide

The number one reason people offer for choosing assisted suicide is that they fear losing autonomy, or control over their bodies and lives.

Death and Dying in America

The average life expectancy in the United States is 78 years old. The RAND Institute estimates that 40 percent of American deaths are preceded by a period of dementia and enfeeblement that lasts up to 10 years.

Complications

In 2007, there were 3 complications among people who ended their lives using the Death with Dignity Act. None of these was the result of a person changing their mind at the last minute, but they did prolong or otherwise complicate the death process.

Eligibility for Death with Dignity

In order to receive assisted suicide in Oregon, a person must be terminally ill with less than six months to live, be mentally competent and able to make his or her own medical decisions, and be evaluated by two separate doctors. A patient is then given a prescription for a lethal medication, which the patient self-administers—a doctor does not directly give the lethal dose.

Overview

Physician-assisted suicide is among the more recent social issues, although it is debated with as much passion and opinion as older, more classic ones, such as the death penalty or abortion. Why someone would seek help in committing suicide may seem confusing, and in fact this constitutes a large part of the controversy surrounding the practice. Why people want to die, the meaning and value of life, and who should determine the time and place of death (humans, nature, or God) are all critical issues in the assisted suicide debate. To understand them, it is important to appreciate the scope of assisted suicide: where it is practiced, who can access it, and what it offers the terminally ill and suffering.

What Is Physician-Assisted Suicide?

It is necessary to understand the difference between physician-assisted suicide (PAS) and euthanasia, an umbrella term used to describe a variety of forms of death. The term euthanasia comes from a Greek word, which literally means "a good death" or "dying well." In practice, it refers to a scenario in which a doctor either directly causes death or directly allows a death to take place. For example, voluntary euthanasia means that a doctor, at the patient's request, will inject that patient with a lethal substance. Passive euthanasia means that the doctor lets the patient die by removing him or her from life support or withholding other life-saving treatments.

Physician-assisted suicide is neither of these things. In physician-assisted suicide, the doctor neither directly causes the death of a patient nor indirectly causes death by withholding care. Rather, the doctor merely puts the tools of death—in most cases, a prescription for a lethal dose of a medication—in the hands of a patient and leaves the ending of life to the patient's discretion.

Physician-Assisted Suicide Around the World

Physician-assisted suicide is explicitly legal in just four places in the world: The Netherlands, Switzerland, and the states of Oregon and Washington.*

In Oregon assisted suicide is legal under the Death with Dignity Act, which was passed by voters first in 1994 and put into action in 1997. In Switzerland the practice has been legal for much longer, since 1941. The Netherlands officially legalized assisted suicide nationwide in 2002, but it was permitted in various forms by courts beginning in 1984.

> " Why people want to die, the meaning and value of life, and who should determine the time and place of death (humans, nature, or God) are all critical issues in the assisted suicide debate. "

The rules governing assisted suicide are slightly different in each place where it is legal. For example, in Oregon a patient must have a terminal illness in order to qualify for assisted suicide; neither the Netherlands nor Switzerland require this. Both Oregon and the Netherlands require at least 2 physicians to consult on each assisted suicide case; Switzerland does not have this requirement. Likewise, patients seeking death in Oregon and the Netherlands must make repeated requests for assisted suicide (to demonstrate their desire to die is not temporary or

* As this volume went to press, Washington citizens in 2008 voted to legalize assisted suicide there.

fleeting). In all 3 places physician-assisted suicides constitute a very slim minority of all deaths. In Oregon about 0.15 percent of deaths are a result of PAS. The same is true in the Netherlands, where 0.1 percent of deaths result from PAS. Switzerland has a slightly higher rate of about 0.2 percent, which is still statistically small.

> **The rules governing assisted suicide are slightly different in each place where it is legal.**

These three places are the only areas in which assisted suicide is explicitly legal. Other countries have a less clear policy on assisted suicide. Sweden, for example, does not have a law that specifically prohibits assisted suicide, nor does Finland, Denmark, France, or Luxembourg. In Germany, assisted suicide carries no explicit punishment, though euthanasia is listed as a crime. People who have assisted in suicides in these countries are sometimes prosecuted for another kind of crime, such as manslaughter, failing to help a person in trouble, or inappropriately using drugs.

In Canada, Hungary, Italy, New Zealand, Norway, Russia, and the United Kingdom, it is illegal for anyone to assist in a suicide. In Hungary, assisting a suicide is punishable by up to 5 years in prison; in the United Kingdom, the punishment is 14 years. Growing movements in these nations, however, are working to overturn these laws. Organizations such as the Right to Die Society of Canada and the UK-based Dignity in Dying are increasingly active in their quest to legalize assisted suicide.

In Japan, where some forms of suicide are viewed as a ritual act that can restore honor to a shamed person, some forms of euthanasia are legal, though exceedingly rare. Interestingly, Japan has the largest right-to-die group in the whole world; the Japan Society for Dying with Dignity boasts more than 100,000 members. Assisted suicide has had a spotty history in Australia, too: The practice was legal in the Northern Territory of Australia for 7 months until the federal government banned it nationwide in 1997. In that time just 4 people used it.

Perhaps the most nebulous law is in Belgium, where in 2002 a new law legalized euthanasia but not assisted suicide specifically. Although Belgians do not use the term *assisted suicide,* doctors are allowed to cause death by giving a lethal injection at the patient's request or by prescribing a lethal overdose. Yet because they do not explicitly call the practice assisted suicide, and because it is available only under certain conditions, Belgium is only sometimes counted among nations where the practice is explicitly legal.

How a Person Might Use Assisted Suicide

But why would someone need a doctor's help in committing suicide? This question is an integral part of the assisted suicide debate and has many answers. Supporters of assisted suicide claim that allowing a doctor to provide a dying patient with a lethal dose of medication offers the individual a compassionate, dignified way of dying. Indeed, while anyone can commit suicide on their own, doing so is often a violent, painful experience. Certainly, hanging, shooting, or stabbing oneself results in a death that is exceedingly painful, not to mention horrible for loved ones to witness or discover. The idea behind physician-assisted suicide, therefore, is to give people who are going to die soon anyway a painless, peaceful way to exit the world.

But laws such as Oregon's Death with Dignity Act require that individuals meet several requirements before they are allowed this peaceful exit. Under that law they must be diagnosed with a terminal illness and given 6 months or less to live. This means that a person who is terribly disfigured, confined to a wheelchair, or languishing in a coma would be ineligible for PAS. A more likely candidate is someone with lung cancer who is told by her doctor she has 3 or 4 months left to live. After this diagnosis, she can ask her doctor for assisted suicide.

> " Why would someone need a doctor's help in committing suicide? This question is an integral part of the assisted suicide debate and has many answers. "

Once someone has made a request for physician-assisted suicide, the *diagnosis*—the determination of what illness the patient has—and the *prognosis*—the length of time the patient is expected to live—must be agreed upon by a second doctor. It is thought that requiring two doctors to be part of the process helps make diagnoses and prognoses as accurate as possible. The patient is also required to make three requests for PAS, at least one in writing. These requests must

Ray Carnay of Eugene, Oregon, who was diagnosed with throat cancer and given six months to live, sits with his 100 capsules of Seconal, a lethal dose of sleeping pills. When his pain becomes too great, he says, he will take the pills and die peacefully.

convince doctors that no family member or friend has talked the patient into suicide—the decision to die must be the decision of the patient alone.

The patient must also be deemed to be mentally competent, capable of making rational, independent decisions. This is to avoid acting on hasty decisions made by people suffering from temporary depression or mental instability. A patient suspected of being depressed must be referred to a mental health counselor for an evaluation, and the request for PAS can be denied at this point. Other rules governing assisted suicide under the Death with Dignity Act include the requirements that a person has to be a resident of Oregon and can take back the request for lethal medication at any time.

In the most common physician-assisted suicide scenario, a dying patient receives a prescription for a lethal dose of a drug from a doctor after fulfilling all the requirements of the law. The patient may fill the prescription immediately, or hold off, taking time to ponder the enormity of the decision. After obtaining the medication from a pharmacist, the patient may decide to hold on to it for a while. At some point, in a somber ceremony surrounded by relatives, loved ones, and possibly the doctor who prescribed the medication, the patient may take the medication and drift off to a painless death. Or, as in nearly half of all assisted suicide cases in Oregon, the person may still choose to die a natural death, comforted by the knowledge that a painless escape is just a medicine cabinet away.

Assisted Suicide as a "Pro-Choice" Issue

Assisted suicide is often lumped together with other bioethics issues, such as abortion. Supporters of one tend to be supporters of the other, finding consistency in arguments related to personal freedom and choice. The points commonly made in favor of legalizing abortion, for example, tend to center around women's right to have control over their own bodies. Supporters of assisted suicide adopt a similar line of logic: that the people's right to have control over their own bodies applies not just to the manner in which they live but also to how they die. For example, a 2007 Harris Poll that compared support for various social issues found that the majority of Democrats—66 percent—support abortion rights. A smaller majority of Democrats, 40 percent, also support assisted suicide. (In this instance, 29 percent opposed assisted suicide while 31 percent were unsure about it.) In a similar show of issue loyalty, the same poll showed exactly 31 percent of Republicans favoring both abortion and assisted suicide.

> " Supporters of assisted suicide believe that the people's right to have control over their own bodies applies not just to the manner in which they live but also to how they die. "

That people who support other social issues such as abortion should also support assisted suicide is frequently suggested by people such as Lennard Davis, professor of disability studies at the University of Illinois. Davis and others warn disability rights groups against opposing assisted suicide on the grounds that it contradicts their stake in supporting other issues that are important to them. "Most disability activists support a liberal agenda; support a right to choice," reasons Davis. "The downside to taking the strong stance that Not Dead Yet [an anti-assisted-suicide group] takes is that it associates people with disabilities with a right-wing agenda. Are they going to be marching again tomorrow with people against gay marriage? Against abortion? Against the right to privacy?"[1] Republicans, too, find similarities between the two issues, and this has been the reason they have nicknamed Democrats "The Party of Death."

Certainly, the two issues have some similarities. Personal autonomy is a prevailing argument for both why women should be able to dictate the terms of their pregnancies and also why terminally ill persons should be allowed to end their lives if they decide life is no longer worth living. That legalizing both abortion and assisted suicide keeps it safe and regulated is another argument shared by the two issues. For example, when abortion was illegal, women did not refrain from having them—they were simply forced to visit outlaw doctors who would overcharge and perform the procedure, often in unsanitary surgical conditions. Legalizing abortion, therefore, ensured that women who were going to have abortions anyway could do so in a safe and controlled environment.

> "Supporters of assisted suicide argue that keeping it illegal only forces people to take their lives violently and in violation of the law."

In the same way, supporters of assisted suicide argue that keeping it illegal only forces people to take their lives violently and in violation of the law. Indeed, stories abound of terminally ill people who are denied access to assisted suicide shooting themselves, jumping off bridges, suffocating themselves, or attempting suicide in other ways that are dangerous, undignified, or unduly violent. Worse, they are sometimes forced to implicate their family members in their own murder if they are physically unable to kill themselves on their own. If they are successful, their benefactors are likely to be denied insurance payouts, since most insurance companies do not honor policies in the event of suicide (which is not the case in Oregon, where the survivors of people who die under the Death with Dignity Act remain entitled to insurance payouts since Death with Dignity Act deaths are not considered by the law to be true suicides). If they are unsuccessful, they run the risk of maim-

Debbie Purdy, who suffers from multiple sclerosis, arrives at court in 2008 to see if her husband (kneeling at right) will face charges if he helps her when she decides to end her life due to pain from her illness.

ing themselves, making life even more unbearable for them. For all of these reasons, outlawing an action that people seem determined to do regardless of the law seems petty and useless. As journalist Robert Lake writes, "Prohibition didn't work with booze or abortions. Regulating euthanasia sounds dreadful, but it may prevent desperate people grievously maiming themselves by going it alone or aided by quacks."[2]

"Autonomy Is an Illusion"

Yet others find no value in linking assisted suicide with abortion and other bioethics issues, mainly because they reject the suggestion that assisted suicide has anything to do with personal autonomy. Some cynically argue that physician-assisted suicide puts not the patient in control, but doctors and the profit-driven medical industry, which surely would prefer the inexpensive death of patients rather than the expensive prolonged care of them. Still others claim that if patients had better end-of-life (or palliative) care, they would be just as happy to make choices that related to the extension of their lives rather than their deaths. Such a perspective comes from psychiatry professor Herbert Hendlin, who says, "Patient autonomy is an illusion when physicians are not trained to assess and treat patient suffering."[3] If doctors were able to offer their terminally ill patients more choices, in other words, the patients would not feel empowered by the prospect of taking their own lives.

> ❝ Opponents reject the assumption that wanting to commit suicide, for any reason, is a rational choice that people should have a right to make. ❞

Perhaps most often, however, opponents reject the assumption that wanting to commit suicide, for any reason, is a rational choice that people should have a right to make. Rather, they view any suicidal desire as the result of depression, lack of other options, or another remediable cause. Cardinal Bernard Law, the former Archbishop of Boston, expresses this idea in the following way:

> Supporters claim that assisted suicide is about promoting "freedom of choice" and relieving suffering for terminally ill people. Yet people who may want to commit suicide are found in every demographic group—especially among the young, the very old and members of high-stress professions. Suicidal desires among the terminally ill are no more "free," and no less caused by treatable depression, than those felt by other people. Yet an entire political movement has dedicated itself to facilitating suicide for the seriously ill, even while the law rightly continues to forbid this destructive "choice" for everyone else.[4]

In this way, linking death with the rights granted in life is, for those opposed to legalization, very much beyond the scope of the U.S. Constitution. In fact, this was a main reason the Supreme Court in 1997 ruled that Americans do not have a constitutionally protected right to commit suicide. The Court, like many Americans, did not find merit in protecting a person's ability to end life, a cherished, valued thing, the protection of which is at the very cornerstone of civilized society. Nor did it find that suicide or assisted suicide was consistent with other rights guaranteed in the Constitution. Interestingly, all of the times in which the Supreme Court has ruled in support of Oregon's Death with Dignity Act, it has not done so because it sanctioned suicide or assisted suicide, but because it agreed that the Oregon voters had the right to shape their state's laws so long as they are not in direct violation of the Constitution (a notion called "state's rights").

Finally, a key difference between assisted suicide and other bioethics issues is the number of people who benefit from legalization. In the United States, for example, more than 1 million women exercise their right to access abortion services each year. In contrast, only about 40 Oregonians use the Death with Dignity Act to end their lives each year. That so few people use assisted suicide has caused some Americans to question whether it is all that important to fight for the right to access it. Or, as professor Kevin Yuill puts it, "Looked at simply in practical terms, it is difficult to understand why this is not an obscure issue of medical ethics"[5] rather than the impassioned sociopolitical debate it has become. Yuill says that if assisted suicide were to become legal in the United Kingdom, only about 650 people a year would probably take advantage of it. "This is fairly insignificant compared with the 4,629 persons that committed suicide in England and Wales in 2003, let alone the total in 2004 of 514,250 deaths," he points out. "Even if the legislation were enacted, only a very small number of people—somewhere near a tenth of the total suicides every year—would avail themselves of the option."[6] For Yuill and others, it is not worth legalizing assisted suicide for so few people to use, especially when doing so could open the door to so many risks.

> " The Court, like many Americans, did not find merit in protecting a person's ability to end life, a cherished, valued thing. "

Thus far, because assisted suicide is specifically or tacitly prohibited in so many countries, most debates about assisted suicide are only theoretical. Yet these debates remain relevant because of the increasingly powerful organizations dedicated to legalizing assisted suicide around the globe and in the United States. Whether they will succeed in legalizing the practice in more places remains unseen, but it is clear that the ethics, parameters, and risks of assisted suicide will be a continued feature of social debate throughout the twenty-first century.

Is Assisted Suicide Moral?

> 66 If death is in a patient's best interest, then death constitutes a moral good. 99
>
> —Len Doyal and Lesley Doyal, professors of medical ethics, health, and social care.

> 66 Legalizing [physician-assisted suicide] would harm the very important shared societal value of respect for life, and change the basic norm that we must not kill one another. 99
>
> —Margaret Somerville, director of the Centre for Medicine, Ethics, and Law at McGill University.

B ecause assisted suicide involves the monumental issues of life, death, and the meaning and nature of both, its morality has been hotly debated by philosophers, ethicists, lawyers, clergy people, and religious Americans. Often a person's opinion about whether physician-assisted suicide is moral is determined by his or her religious, spiritual, or humanitarian convictions about the value and purpose of life, human rights, and the nature of death. Sometimes people decide whether physician-assisted suicide is moral based on the degree of suffering it relieves, the effect it has on the doctor-patient relationship, whether it offers an ill person the chance to die with dignity and compassion, and whether it honors or devalues life itself.

Is It Ever Moral to Condone Suicide and Killing?

Some ground their opposition to physician-assisted suicide in spiritual traditions that view both killing and suicide as immoral. Rationales for these positions are frequently found in religious doctrines, most famously the sixth commandment, which states, "Thou shall not kill." Indeed, Judaism, Christianity, and Islam all either forbid suicide or view it as a grave sin, and Hindus regard killing oneself as serious a crime as killing another person. For these reasons, many countries have at one point in their history designated suicide as an illegal act. In the United States, suicide was listed as a felony in states as recently as the late twentieth century (though no one has ever been punished for attempting it). Still, both religious and legal understandings of suicide and murder have typically deemed both actions to be taboo across the globe and throughout time.

But supporters of physician-assisted suicide point out that killing is not always frowned upon by society, nor is it always deemed wrong. Just as the police make exceptions when they shoot criminals, or the military makes exceptions when soldiers are asked to kill in times of war, so too do people believe moral exceptions should be made in the field of medicine when it comes to end-of-life matters. As psychology professor Robert Lake puts it, "[Critics of physician-assisted suicide say] it's wrong to kill another human. It certainly is, but that argument pursued zealously means we should disband the Canadian Armed Forces. Regrettably, armies sooner or later kill. Regrettably, police do too. We hope they do reluctantly and rarely, but we sanction their killings."[7] For Lake and others who support physician-assisted suicide, both killing and suicide are appropriate at certain times; and if these actions are taken in the context of care, humanitarian justice, and duty, they constitute moral behavior.

> " **Judaism, Christianity, and Islam all either forbid suicide or view it as a grave sin, and Hindus regard killing oneself as serious a crime as killing another person.** "

Still others consider physician-assisted suicide to count neither as murder *nor* suicide. Since physician-assisted suicide occurs with a person's consent, and most often constitutes the hastening of death in patients who are going to die soon anyway, the practice's supporters make a point of distinguishing the act from situations in which people end their otherwise healthy and potential-filled lives, or from situations in which people have had their lives taken from them against their will. For them, physician-assisted suicide is so removed from traditional forms of killing and suicide that they prefer to call the act "physician aid in dying" or "hastened death." Explains psychiatry professor Wesley Sowers,

> Suicide signifies the premature, self-inflicted termination of a life that has not yet exhausted its potential. In the case of assisted dying, a person whose death is inevitable within a short period of time chooses the time and circumstances of their death. It is a considered rational response to avoid suffering associated with the meaningless extension of a life that has essentially reached its conclusion."[8]

Yet for those who oppose physician-assisted suicide, such distinctions are hair-splitting euphemisms that contribute to an unnatural, and thus immoral, death.

> " Supporters of physician-assisted suicide point out that killing is not always frowned upon by society, nor is it always deemed wrong. "

The Doctor-Patient Relationship

How physician-assisted suicide affects the doctor-patient relationship is another question raised when one grapples with the morality of the practice. Arguments against physician-assisted suicide frequently involve the Hippocratic Oath, an ancient pledge taken by doctors that calls for them to use their skills for healing rather than harm. The Hippocratic Oath requires a doctor to promise to "benefit my patients according to my greatest ability and judgment, and I will do no harm or injustice to them. I will not give a lethal drug to anyone if I am asked, nor will I advise such a plan."[9] Those opposed to physician-assisted suicide, therefore, believe doctors who help patients end their lives are in fundamental opposition to their job as healers.

Physicians for Compassionate Care is a group comprised of doctors who oppose physician-assisted suicide for exactly this reason. They oppose the practice on the grounds that it is at odds with a doctor's job to heal. In their view, doctors who engage in the practice amount to part-time executioners, and thus, "Doctor assisted suicide undermines trust in the patient-physician relationship; changes the role of the physician in society from the traditional role of healer to that of the executioner; [and] endangers the value that society places on life, especially for those who are most vulnerable and who are near the end of life."[10]

Not only are opponents concerned about the effect of PAS on the doctor-patient relationship, but concern has been raised for doctors themselves who have participated in the practice. Some studies have shown that doctors who have helped patients die later exhibit remorse and isolation. Says one doctor who has extensively studied the effects of participating in physician-assisted suicide cases on Oregon doctors: "There is a huge burden on conscience, tangled emotions and a large psychological toll on the participating physicians."[11] The American Medical Association (AMA) officially condemns physician-assisted suicide as "fundamentally inconsistent with the physician's professional role."[12] As a result, the organization instructs doctors to refuse to participate in assisted suicide cases, and instead urges them to focus on end-of-life care and comfort.

> " How physician-assisted suicide affects the doctor-patient relationship is another question raised when one grapples with the morality of the practice. "

A Doctor's Duty to Relieve Suffering

Yet plenty of doctors and patients disagree with the AMA, viewing physician-assisted suicide as a compassionate act that complements a doctor's role as a caregiver. While the Hippocratic Oath does bind a physician to treat rather than harm patients, it can be argued that offering the terminally, suffering ill a swift, dignified passing at the time of their choosing falls within the bounds of such caring treatment. As philosophy professor Michael B. Gill put it in his defense of Oregon's Death with Dignity Act, "In caring for dying patients, one of a physician's principal roles is to reduce suffering. When healing is no longer possible, the reduction of suffering takes center stage."[13] For Gill and others, physician-assisted suicide qualifies as a moral way to reduce suffering if the patient chooses it.

Furthermore, some point out that the Hippocratic Oath is not meant to be taken as literally as those who oppose PAS do. After all, it must be remembered that the Hippocratic Oath first instructed doctors to "do no harm" sometime prior to the fourth century B.C. when the field of medicine often overlapped with sorcery, alchemy, and other practices from which true medicine needed to distinguish itself. Indeed, other pieces of the Hippocratic Oath have ceased to be relevant in most contemporary Western nations, such as the part that binds doctors not to "give a woman means to procure an abortion."[14] However, in nations where abortion has been determined to be a woman's right, a matter of public health, and a personal moral choice, the literal application of this and other parts of the oath have been discarded. As medical ethicist Daniel Sokol says, "It is therefore wrong slavishly to revere—as some still do—the Hippocratic Oath. If taken literally, the only way doctors could 'do no harm' would be by declining to treat all patients. Even simple medical procedures, such as taking a blood sample or injecting a local anesthetic, entail some risks to the patient."[15] Instead of interpreting the Hippocratic Oath so strictly, most doctors understand it as binding them to treat patients to the best of their ability and in the patients' best interests. For doctors who believe that the terminally ill should be allowed to choose to die in a safe, dignified manner, physician-assisted suicide is not in conflict with the oath they have taken.

> "Those opposed to physician-assisted suicide believe doctors who help patients end their lives are in fundamental opposition to their job as healers."

That physician-assisted suicide is consistent with a doctor's role is also reflected in public polls, which show majority levels of support for the practice among both doctors and patients. A February 2007 national survey of physicians, for example, found the majority—57 percent—believe it is ethical to assist an individual who has made a rational choice to die as a result of unbearable suffering. Patients also find room for the practice in a doctor's job description: A 2005 study reported in the *Journal of Medical Ethics* found that just 20 percent of survey respondents said they would trust their doctor less if he or she were allowed to help patients die. Conversely, 58 percent said they would maintain trust in their doctor. "Despite the widespread concern that legalizing physician-assisted death would seriously threaten or undermine trust in physicians," said lead researcher Mark Hall, "the weight of the evidence in the United States is to the contrary."[16]

A Dignified, Compassionate Death?

Terminally ill people rarely die swiftly and painlessly. More often, their deaths are prolonged, painful experiences that render them incontinent, dependent on others, a prisoner of their own bodies. Because of this, supporters believe that allowing someone to hasten his or her own death via physician-assisted suicide offers a terminally ill person the chance to die a compassionate, dignified death. In this way, they view the practice as a moral, humane act that relieves suffering and honors life.

One man described the assisted death of his friend Joe as reflecting this compassion, saying, "Joe was a handsome man, tall and straight, a dignified presence in any gathering. He chose to leave the world at his good time with his family at his side. I write to thank those citizens who voted for Oregon's Death with Dignity law. Because of them my friend Joe finished life with his self-control and dignity unspoiled."[17] Like Joe, hundreds of people in Oregon, Switzerland, and the Netherlands, where assisted suicide is legal, have viewed hastened death as a gift that lets them exit the world while they can still say goodbye to their loved ones with all their faculties intact. In contrast, New Yorker Yomery Santana describes how her state's lack of an assisted suicide law kept her terminally ill mother suffering much longer than necessary: "If I only knew my mom

> " For doctors who believe that the terminally ill should be allowed to choose to die in a safe, dignified manner, physician-assisted suicide is not in conflict with the oath they have taken. "

would endure so much pain before she parted, I would [have] opted to move to Oregon to exercise her right to die in peace. My 39-year-old mom had terminal cancer and endured the slowest, most devastating painful dying process I have ever seen. She would ask God to take her, that's how bad it had gotten."[18]

However, PAS opponents argue that while alleviating suffering sounds like a noble enough reason to legalize the practice, in reality very few patients actually elect PAS because they are in unbearable pain. Rather, most do so before they get to this point, citing a desire to have control over their deaths, avoid becoming a burden to their families, avoid losing autonomy, or avoid losing their dignity—reasons that opponents of PAS believe are able to be addressed with better end-of-life care. Says Wesley J. Smith, attorney for the International Task Force on Euthanasia and Assisted Suicide, "These are all important issues, and it is incumbent upon doctors to help patients overcome them. But they do not reflect the severe physical suffering the AAHPM [American Academy of Hospice and Palliative Measures] presumes would cause their patients to request assisted suicide."[19] In the view of Smith and others, society should not be allowing people to prematurely end their lives when there is much the medical community can do to help them.

> "While alleviating suffering sounds like a noble enough reason to legalize the practice, in reality very few patients actually elect PAS because they are in unbearable pain."

The Value of Life

And even if physicians can do nothing to stave off the inevitable, opponents of physician-assisted suicide insist that whenever the taking of a life is sanctioned, the value of human life becomes fundamentally diminished. They insist that life is too precious for humans to snuff out when they see fit, or believe that only God can decide when it is time for life to end if the gift of life is to have any meaning at all. As Margaret Somerville, director of the Centre for Medicine, Ethics, and Law at McGill University puts it, "Might the strongest argument against [physician-assisted suicide] relate not to death but to life? That is, the argument that normalizing it would destroy a sense of the unfathomable mystery of life and seriously damage our human spirit, especially our capacity to find meaning in life."[20]

But the claim that assisted suicide devalues life is attacked by those who point out that not everyone shares the same standard of the value of life in the first place. Or, as Lake puts it, "We all know what human life is, except we all know something different."[21] This perspective illuminates the difficulty of saying for sure whether life is ultimately devalued or honored by physician-assisted suicide—one person's life worth living may be another person's life worth ending. Determining whether physician-assisted suicide is moral or compassionate is an intensely personal decision to which there is no universal answer. The value of life, along with other ethical topics related to physician-assisted suicide, will remain a point of moral contention, and one that perhaps can be determined only by individuals and their families when they face death themselves.

> **The claim that assisted suicide devalues life is attacked by those who point out that not everyone shares the same standard of the value of life in the first place.**

Primary Source Quotes*

Is Assisted Suicide Moral?

> **❝If doctors and others are faithfully to benefit the life the patient still has, they cannot sit in ultimate judgment of its worth, and cannot ever think that lethal intervention is an acceptable 'therapeutic option.'❞**
>
> —Eric Cohen and Leon R. Kass, "'Cast Me Not Off in Old Age,'" *Commentary*, January 2006, pp. 32–38.
>
> Cohen is the director of the program in biotechnology and American democracy at the Ethics and Public Policy Center. Kass is a professor in the Committee on Social Thought at the University of Chicago.

> **❝Physician-assisted suicide can be compatible with love, kindness and compassion.❞**
>
> —Daniel Sokol, "The Ethics of Assisted Suicide," British Broadcasting Company, May 11, 2006.
>
> Sokol is a medical ethicist and coauthor of *Medical Ethics and Law: Surviving on the Wards and Passing Exams.*

Bracketed quotes indicate conflicting positions.

* Editor's Note: While the definition of a primary source can be narrowly or broadly defined, for the purposes of Compact Research, a primary source consists of: 1) results of original research presented by an organization or researcher; 2) eyewitness accounts of events, personal experience, or work experience; 3) first-person editorials offering pundits' opinions; 4) government officials presenting political plans and/or policies; 5) representatives of organizations presenting testimony or policy.

66 **Physician assisted suicide is fundamentally inconsistent with the physician's professional role. . . . Requests for physician assisted suicide should be a signal to the physician that the patient's needs are unmet.** 99

—American Medical Association, "Physician Assisted Suicide," Policy H-140.952. www.ama-assn.org.

The AMA is the largest association of doctors and medical students in the United States.

66 **Against the background of the duty to care, the moral and legal status of not saving a life through failing to treat can be the same as actively taking that life. . . . Provided the circumstances are clinically warranted, doctors should be able to withdraw life sustaining treatment when they intend to accelerate death as well as to relieve suffering.** 99

—Len Doyal and Lesley Doyal, "Why Active Euthanasia and Physician Assisted Suicide Should Be Legalized," *British Medical Journal,* vol. 323, November 10, 2001, p. 1,079.

Len Doyal is professor of medical ethics at the University of London. Lesley Doyal is professor of health and social care at the University of Bristol.

66 **[Physician-assisted suicide] abandons patients—whose lives depend on ethical doctors acting energetically to relieve suffering while abiding by the Hippocratic Oath's sacred duty to 'neither give a deadly drug to anybody who asked for it, nor . . . make a suggestion to this effect.'** 99

—Wesley J. Smith, "First, Do Harm . . . A Betrayal of the Hospice Movement," *Weekly Standard,* vol. 12, no. 26, March 19, 2007.

Smith is an attorney for the International Task Force on Euthanasia and Assisted Suicide and a consultant to the Center for Bioethics and Culture.

❝There is an obvious problem with claiming that trying to make patients healthy is a physician's only moral duty. The problem is that people with terminal diseases cannot be made healthy. . . . No one advocates that physicians are obligated by their professional ethic to abandon their patients upon making a terminal diagnosis. On the contrary, it is well recognized that physicians have especially pressing obligations to such patients' care.❞

—Michael B. Gill, "A Moral Defense of Oregon's Physician-Assisted Suicide Law," *Mortality,* vol. 10, no. 1, February 2005, p. 61. www.u.arizona.edu.

Gill is a professor of philosophy at the University of Arizona, Tucson.

❝If the end is to be like that of my grandfather or his daughter, my mother, I may choose to end the suffering, the terrible financial and emotional drain that my family will inevitably endure. I don't know—yet. But I would like to have a choice.❞

—Quoted in Karen Hwang, "Attitudes of Persons with Physical Disabilities Toward Physician-Assisted Death: An Exploratory Assessment of the Vulnerability Argument," *Journal of Disability Policy Studies,* vol. 16, no. 1, Summer 2005, p. 16.

This quotation is from an anonymous member of New Mobility, a group dedicated to disability culture and lifestyle.

❝What message is conveyed to our children if we choose to dispense with a terminally ill loved one rather than offering them the comfort and reassurance they need at their most difficult hour?❞

—Nancy Murray, "Terminally Ill Need Love, Reassurance," *Tri-City Herald* (Pasco, WA), July 20, 2008, p. F1.

Murray is a columnist for the *Tri-City Herald,* a newspaper in Pasco, Washington.

> 66 The experiences I've had with people who have used this law have been inspiring. In most cases, the family is nearby. The patient is rarely in tears. What happens when people are dying is they start withdrawing from what is around them. They focus on getting emotional business done. They focus on what is beyond, and when they go, all the pieces are aligned. 99

—Teresa Grove, quoted in Kathie Durbin, "For Assisted Suicide: Teresa Grove," *McClatchy-Tribune Business News,* July 13, 2008.

Grove is a hospice nurse who works with the group Compassion and Choices, which assists people in dying.

> 66 While I can recall only one family that requested assisted suicide, I could not begin to count how many have experienced love and healing and wonderful closure. It would be wrong for us to offer the option of preempting this process. It is as much a part of life as birth, and we should not actively interfere with it. 99

—Robert Woodson, testimony regarding Senate Bill 151 before the Wisconsin State Senate Committee on Public Health, Senior Issues, Long Term Care and Privacy, January 23, 2008. www.cmdahome.org.

Woodson is a professor of medicine at the University of Wisconsin School of Medicine and Public Health.

> 66 We all have a private right to suicide. . . . Assisted suicide brings another person into the act. . . . It is not appropriate to bring another person into a suicide. 99

—Richard Radtke, "A Case Against Physician-Assisted Suicide," *Journal of Disability Policy Studies,* vol. 16, no. 1, Summer 2005, p. 58.

Radtke is the founder of Sea of Dreams Foundation, a disability rights organization. He is also a quadriplegic.

❝ Calls for assisted suicide arise at the intersection of human despair and political opportunity. The absence of a Christian worldview leaves personal autonomy as the foundation of ethical choice. Death becomes, of all things, a matter of individual rights. The only real alternative to this logic is the framework of the biblical worldview—a worldview that understands every single human life to be sacred, every individual to possess full human dignity, all life to be a stewardship, and death to be a matter for God, not we ourselves, to decide. ❞

—Albert Mohler, "A Threat to the Disabled . . . and to Us All," AlbertMohler.com, August 9, 2007.

Mohler is president of the Southern Baptist Theological Seminary and a leader among American evangelicals.

❝ There is no rational, secular basis upon which the government can properly prevent any individual from choosing to end his own life. When religious conservatives use secular laws to enforce their faith in God, they threaten the central principle on which America was founded. ❞

—Thomas A. Bowden, "Assisted Suicide: A Moral Right," *Capitalism Magazine,* March 27, 2005. www.capmag.com.

Bowden is a writer for the Ayn Rand Institute, a think tank that promotes the principles of reason, rational self-interest, and individual rights.

Facts and Illustrations

Is Assisted Suicide Moral?

- According to the Oregon Department of Human Services:
  - **Forty-five** doctors participated in assisted suicides in 2007.
  - During 2007, **no physicians** who participated in the DWDA were referred to the Oregon Medical Board for inappropriate or suspicious conduct.
  - The median length of the doctor-patient relationship of people who use assisted suicide is **11 weeks,** though relationships range from **0 to1,440** weeks.
  - A prescribing physician was present at the time of death in **27.9 percent** of assisted suicide cases.
  - Another kind of health-care provider was present in **52.8 percent** of cases.
  - No provider was present in **19.2 percent** of cases.

- According to a 2005 study published in the *Journal of Medical Ethics:*
  - **58 percent** of people said that legalized physician-assisted suicide would not cause them to trust their doctor less.
  - **20 percent** said legalized physician-assisted suicide would cause them to trust their doctor less.
  - **27 percent** of adults 65 and older said they would be more likely to distrust their doctor if physician-assisted suicide was legal.
  - **32 percent** of black Americans said they would be more likely to distrust their doctor if physician-assisted suicide was legal.

Pharmacist Opinions on Lethal Medication Prescriptions

Pharmacists have increasingly voiced their opinion on whether to fill controversial prescriptions, such as birth control pills or abortifacients (a medication that causes an abortion). Whether they would be willing to dispense lethal doses of medications is of growing debate as more states consider legalizing assisted suicide.

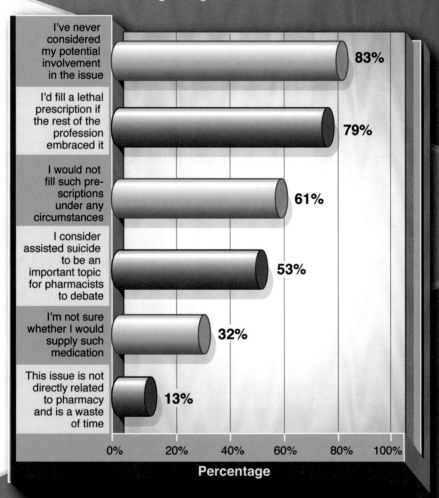

	Percentage
I've never considered my potential involvement in the issue	83%
I'd fill a lethal prescription if the rest of the profession embraced it	79%
I would not fill such pre-scriptions under any circumstances	61%
I consider assisted suicide to be an important topic for pharmacists to debate	53%
I'm not sure whether I would supply such medication	32%
This issue is not directly related to pharmacy and is a waste of time	13%

Note: Does not total 100 percent because pharmacists could select more than one answer.

Source: Royal Pharmaceutical Society of Great Britain, "Pharmacy and Assisted Suicide and Euthanasia: International Experience," 2007. www.rpsgb.org.uk.

- According to psychiatrist Herbert Hendlin, who was given rare access to Dutch files on assisted suicide cases in the Netherlands:
  - **50 percent** of Dutch doctors feel it is appropriate to suggest assisted suicide to their patients.
  - **25 percent** of doctors said they had terminated a patient's life without his or her specific permission.
  - **33 percent** of doctors said they could imagine terminating a patient's life without his or her request.

- A February 2007 survey of 1,088 physicians conducted by the Louis Finkelstein Institute for Social and Religious Research and HCD Research found:
  - **57 percent** of physicians believe that it is ethical to assist an individual who, due to unbearable suffering, has made a rational choice to die.

Public Opinions on the Morality of Assisted Suicide

An annual Gallup poll consistently finds that Americans are nearly evenly divided on whether assisted suicide is moral or not. However, a slight majority believes the practice is moral.

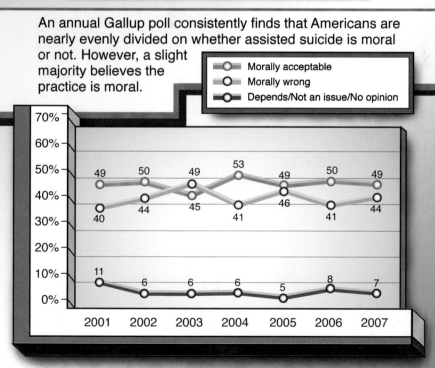

Legend:
- Morally acceptable
- Morally wrong
- Depends/Not an issue/No opinion

	2001	2002	2003	2004	2005	2006	2007
Morally acceptable	49	50	49	53	49	50	49
Morally wrong	40	44	45	41	46	41	44
Depends/Not an issue/No opinion	11	6	6	6	5	8	7

Source: Joseph Carroll, "Public Divided Over Moral Acceptability of Doctor-Assisted Suicide," Gallup.com, May 31, 2007. www.gallup.com.

Religious People Tend to Oppose Assisted Suicide

A 2007 Gallup poll found that people who attend church every week tend to overwhelmingly view assisted suicide as immoral; people who rarely or never attend church, however, tend to view it as moral.

Question: Is physician-assisted suicide morally acceptable?

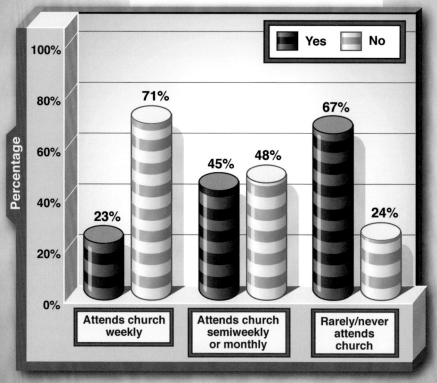

Source: Joseph Caroll, "Public Divided Over Moral Acceptability of Doctor-Assisted Suicide," Gallup.com, May 31, 2007. www.gallup.com.

- **39 percent** believe such assistance is unethical.
- **41 percent** of physicians said they support the legalization of physician-assisted suicide for a wide variety of cases.
- **30 percent** support legalizing physician-assisted suicide in just a few kinds of cases.
- **29 percent** completely oppose its legalization.

- **72 percent** of conservative doctors said they think assisted suicide is unethical.
- **81 percent** of liberal doctors said they think assisted suicide is ethical.
- **66 percent** of conservative doctors oppose legalizing assisted suicide.
- **64 percent** of liberal doctors support legalizing assisted suicide.
- **54 percent** of doctors polled believe that assisted suicide should be a matter between patient and doctor alone.
- **54 percent** of doctors polled believe the government should not regulate the practice.
- **46 percent** said the government should regulate physician-assisted suicide.

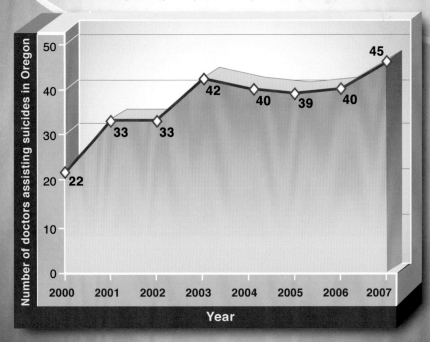

Physician Involvement in the Oregon Death with Dignity Act

Because assisted suicide is such a controversial issue, just a small number of doctors assist in suicides each year in Oregon, where the practice is legal. Polls have shown that even when doctors think assisted suicide is moral, they are reluctant to participate personally in the process.

Source: Oregon Department of Human Services, "Death with Dignity Annual Report: Summary for 2007," March 2008. www.oregon.gov.

Should Assisted Suicide Be Legal?

66 I'd like to know that in a reasonable civil society that this option was available, rather than having my friend having to put a plastic bag over my head or shoot me. And I think most people feel that. **99**

—Lennard Davis, professor of disability studies at the University of Illinois at Chicago.

66 I have received only one request for termination of life. . . . I was not able to figure out how much of this request was truly her own idea and how much she was influenced by her daughters, who were very adamant. **99**

—Dr. Robert Woodson, professor at the University of Wisconsin School of Medicine and Public Health.

B ecause of its controversial nature, physician-assisted suicide has been legalized in just a few places in the world. Despite this, the idea that people should have the right to control the time and manner of their death in the event they are terminally ill or in unbearable pain has appealed to citizens of many countries and states.

The Death with Dignity Act: A Safe and Reasonable Law?

Approved by Oregon voters in 1994 and put into practice in 1997, the Death with Dignity Act (DWDA) legalized physician-assisted suicide in the state of Oregon. Since the act's inception, 341 terminally ill people have used it to end their lives. The main thrust behind the act was to offer terminally ill, suffering people the chance to end their lives before their pain became too great; before they lost bodily functions; before they became an undue burden to their families; and most of all, the chance to die in a dignified manner that reflected and respected the way in which they had lived.

The DWDA has several safeguards in place to prevent the act from being abused. In order to receive a prescription for a lethal medication, the DWDA requires that a person be 18 years old, a resident of Oregon, able to make and communicate health-care decisions, and diagnosed with a terminal disease that will claim his or her life within six months. Furthermore, a person has to be evaluated by two doctors who must concur that the patient is not depressed or mentally ill, and both must agree on the patient's diagnosis. A patient is required to make two requests for the prescription, separated by 15 days. Finally, the patient must be informed of alternatives to suicide, such as hospice care and pain management.

Critics of the DWDA, however, claim these safeguards are easily circumvented, and cite three main problems with the law. First, they argue it is too easy for patients who are temporarily depressed about their condition to receive lethal prescriptions. According to one estimate, fewer than 5 percent of requesting patients in Oregon receive a psychiatric evaluation. And even those who are rejected as a result of their mental condition can continue to make the request until they find a doctor who agrees. "Take the case of Helen, an 80-year-old woman with breast cancer," writes neurologist Kathleen M. Foley. "Her primary physician refused her request for assisted suicide. Her second doctor said she was depressed. A third physician and a psychiatrist agreed with the woman's request, and she was aided in death. I have corresponded with the physician who aided her, and he now says that he is not sure that he would have done it if he had had all the information about her."[22]

> Oregon's Death with Dignity Act has several safeguards in place to prevent the act from being abused.

This case raises a second criticism people have of the DWDA: that it allows a doctor to prescribe lethal medication without being intimately familiar with a patient's case. Reports of cases have surfaced in which a doctor who prescribed lethal medication knew the patient for just weeks, heralding questions about whether PAS was truly the correct, or merely the most convenient, course of action. The superficiality of some doctor-patient relationships has been noted by Rita L. Marker and Wesley J. Smith, attorneys for the International Task Force on Euthanasia and Assisted Suicide. They write, "Although a patient's requests for assisted suicide purportedly must span a 15-day period, official Oregon reports indicate that, over the last seven years, some patients have died by suicide having known their assisting doctors for a week or less."[23] Not only can the doctor-patient relationship be alarmingly superficial, but the prescribing physician does not even have to be a medical doctor. It is reported that any licensed doctor—even a dermatologist—can write terminal prescriptions.

> "Critics worry the Death with Dignity Act allows a doctor to prescribe lethal medication without being intimately familiar with a patient's case.

Finally, critics claim the six month rule—that is, the part of the DWDA that requires a person to be so ill that they would be dead within 6 months of receiving a lethal prescription anyway—is unreliable and cuts short peoples' potential to defy even the most dire of prognoses. The most famous example of this problem comes from Michael Freeland, an Oregon man who was prescribed lethal medication because it was determined that his lung cancer would kill him within months—yet it was another 2 years before he finally died of natural causes. Estimating how much time a terminally ill person has left is a notoriously difficult task, especially with noncancerous disease. "Although most cases of Amyotrophic Lateral Sclerosis (ALS, or Lou Gehrig's disease) are terminal within 5 years of diagnosis, some individuals live for many years with the condition,"[24] writes scholar Rhoda Olkin. Examples of people who have long outlived their diagnosis include the famous research scientist Stephen Hawking, who has survived for more than 25 years with ALS. Furthermore, because the DWDA does not authorize investigations into how prognoses are reached, there is no oversight on how doctors come to their conclusions about how much time a patient has remaining. Those who oppose the DWDA say a wrong prognosis can rob a patient of years of time, which is cause enough for them to oppose it.

Should or Do Americans Have a "Right" to Die?

Regardless of the questions that pertain specifically to the DWDA, supporters of physician-assisted suicide see the matter as one of personal freedom and autonomy, not unlike a person's right to determine the course or outcome of any other matter of his or her life. They talk of the practice as being an inverted, yet integral, part of each American's right to life, liberty, and the pursuit of happiness, except that the pursuit of happiness is interpreted as the pursuit of painlessness. Analyst Thomas A. Bowden, a writer for the Ayn Rand Institute, explains: "What if happiness becomes impossible to attain? What if a dread disease, or some other calamity, drains all joy from life, leaving only misery and suffering? The right to life [in these cases] includes and implies the right to commit suicide."[25] For Bowden and others, to deny people the right to end their lives when they see fit is a denial of the fact that their lives are theirs to begin with—a notion that is at odds with the U.S. Constitution.

Still others view the matter as something a secular state—for example, the United States, whose Constitution requires the separation of church and state—has no business weighing in on. Indeed, many arguments against physician-assisted suicide are religious in nature, echoing sentiments that it is wrong to kill, that only God can determine when a life has reached its conclusion, and that life is an infinitely precious gift that deserves to be experienced and respected at any and all stages. Although many find merit and comfort in these views, because these arguments are all grounded in religious concepts, they are not supposed to be used to guide legal decisions. Bowden agrees that arguments against physician-assisted suicide that inherently involve religious conceptions of morality and the value of life have no business influencing the laws of a secular state. "There is no rational, secular basis upon which the government can properly prevent any individual from choosing to end his own life," he writes. "When religious conservatives use secular laws to enforce their faith in God, they threaten the central principle on which America was founded."[26]

> " Estimating how much time a terminally ill person has left is a notoriously difficult task, especially with noncancerous disease. "

But not everyone believes that taking one's life is a right that Americans are entitled to. The Supreme Court, for example, ruled in the 1997 case *Washington v. Glucksberg* that Americans have no constitutionally protected right to commit suicide. The Court, like many Americans, did not find merit in protecting a person's ability to end life, a cherished, valued thing, the protection of which is at the very cornerstone of civilized society. As writer Nancy Murray has put it, "Is this the kind of 'right' we really want to fight for? Have we, as a society, so completely lost our collective mind that we are now defending our 'right' to choose death by lethal drugs?"[27] Many people agree with Murray, arguing that the government and the medical industry should never be in the business of sanctioning any form of unnatural death, suicide, or killing.

In 2006 the Bush administration tried to use this angle to overturn Oregon's assisted suicide law. The administration challenged the Death with Dignity Act on the grounds that it conflicted with the federal Controlled Substance Act, which makes it a crime for doctors to prescribe lethal doses of medicine without a legitimate medical purpose. The Court rejected this claim, though not necessarily because it was convinced of the right of a person to receive physician-assisted suicide. Rather, the Court ruled that the federal government could not use a federal law to overturn a state law that voters had approved. In other words, the case did more to affirm the right of states rather than the right to assisted suicide—but for supporters of the practice, the outcome did just that.

> " Supporters of physician-assisted suicide see the matter as one of personal freedom and autonomy, not unlike a person's right to determine the course or outcome of any other matter of his or her life. "

Respecting Autonomy and Freedom

For supporters of PAS, the matter ultimately comes down to respecting a person's wishes: if terminally ill, suffering patients want to end their lives, the state should not stand in the way of allowing consenting doctors to help them. Such patients have sought this ability in places where PAS remains illegal, such as Great Britain. In that country, Diane Pretty, who suffered from an increasingly worsening case of motor neuron disease, sparked a national controversy when she petitioned the state to let her receive assisted suicide. The government ultimately rejected her request, a decision that was decried by commentators as government paternalism—or when the state pretends it knows what is best for people. "Her own perception of her best interests, and the perception of those who know and love her, have been judicially overruled,"[28] observed professors Len Doyal and Lesley Doyal. Or, as columnist Joan Ryan has distilled the issue, "We don't want the government telling us how to live our lives. Why, then, do we tolerate it telling us how to end them?"[29]

> **Not everyone believes that taking one's life is a right that Americans are entitled to.**

Yet Americans do tolerate—and routinely ask—the government to interfere on their behalf on plenty of matters, argue PAS opponents. Laws that require people to wear seatbelts, prohibit them from smoking in public spaces, or slap warning labels on potentially harmful products are all examples of ways in which the government has been charged with safeguarding public health and safety. If Americans invite the government into their lives in these kinds of efforts to keep them safe, reason PAS opponents, should they not also ask the government to protect them from the ultimate harm of death?

Separating Choice from Coercion

Indeed, opponents warn it is a mistake to view physician-assisted suicide as a matter of choice and liberty, because it overlooks a critical aspect of the debate: that not everyone who might elect physician-assisted suicide is acting freely. Opponents of PAS warn that paving the way for any form of legalized murder is a dangerous precedent that could too easily be used to take advantage of the dying and elderly. They worry that the old and infirm, whose illnesses are likely to be an expensive, time-intensive labor for their family members, might feel pressure to kill themselves to unburden those they have become dependent on. Or, in an even more nefarious scenario, the sick and dying might be talked into receiving assisted suicide so enterprising family members could receive an early inheritance, save money on hospice care, or otherwise benefit from their deaths. Writes columnist Boris Johnson, "It is certainly possible to imagine that, if assisted suicide were legal in [Great Britain], then old, confused and pain-racked people could start protesting that they 'didn't want to be a burden', and their exhausted and demoralized relatives could indeed begin to persuade themselves that this was the best solution."[30]

> " If terminally ill, suffering patients want to end their lives, the state should not stand in the way of allowing consenting doctors to help them. "

One example of someone who may have been coerced into killing herself comes from a 1999 case in Oregon. That year, Kate Cheney, who suffered from Alzheimer's disease and cancer, received physician-assisted suicide. Yet critics of her death argue that Cheney's daughter pushed her mother, and her mother's doctors, into giving her the lethal prescription. This is the only explanation they found for the fact that two doctors initially declined Cheney's request for PAS on the grounds that she was not mentally fit to request it. One of the doctors even noted concern that Cheney "may be influenced by her family's wishes."[31] Attorney Wesley J. Smith, who has written extensively about the Cheney case, believes this is just one example in which a person was pressured into ending his or her life by family members who stood to gain. "In the end, it didn't matter that two independent mental health professionals found familial pressure was being exerted on Cheney; she received the lethal prescription."[32]

Questionable circumstances surrounding a person's request for physician-assisted suicide remains the key reason why opponents believe the practice cannot be likened to other social issues that are argued on the grounds of freedom of choice, such as reproductive rights and abortion. Because it can be difficult to determine whether a person is truly acting out of pressure from family members or their own choice, PAS opponents feel it is safer to ban the practice altogether than run the risk of the sick and elderly—who are already incredibly vulnerable—being taken advantage of in the most permanent of ways.

Preventing Do-It-Yourself Suicides

Yet like the topics of abortion and drugs, some argue that physician-assisted suicide should be legalized in order to keep it safe and regulated. Prohibiting physician-assisted suicide, the argument goes, will not stop people from seeking suicide options. It will merely force them to seek out methods that are dangerous, undignified, or unduly violent. For example, a person who is denied assisted suicide may bring about his or her own death via a gunshot wound, stabbing, or bridge jump, a gruesome, messy death that is anything but peaceful. One woman, Diane, shares how her father, who suffered from terminal lung cancer, violently took his own life in lieu of having a physician to help him do it. "I found him in his room with his head mostly blown off and blood and brain matter scattered all over his room and the hall to the bathroom," Diane recounts. "There is a better way. If this story can help just one person, it is worth the time it takes to type it here. I hope that you can help others to realize that they and their families deserve a less horrible, more dignified way of dying."[33]

Even worse, some suicide attempts may be only partially successful, leaving the victim alive but even more incapacitated than he or she was prior to the suicide attempt. Because repeated surveys reveal that people who show interest in physician-assisted suicide are determined to control their own death, they are unlikely to be deterred by legal measures that prevent them from doing so with a physician's help. Warns psychiatry professor Wesley Sowers, "Without choice and without the possibility of assistance, many people will become desperate, and it will be more likely that a violent, premature death will occur."[34]

> Opponents warn it is a mistake to view physician-assisted suicide as a matter of choice and liberty, because not everyone who might elect it is acting freely.

Furthermore, advocates of PAS claim that legalizing the practice protects family members who help their loved ones end their lives from being tried or jailed for murder or for the aiding and abetting of a suicide—the last thing that terminally ill people who ask for help dying would want. This was the goal of Debbie Purdy, a multiple sclerosis sufferer who in 2008 petitioned the British government to ask that her husband not be prosecuted if he helps her travel abroad to a suicide clinic in Switzerland. "For 14 years I've been in love with this man, he's everything to me, and I'm not about to see him take a risk of prosecution because of something that's happening to me,"[35] says Purdy.

> **Prohibiting physician-assisted suicide will merely force people to seek out methods that are dangerous, undignified, or unduly violent.**

A similar case is found in Marielle Houle, a Montreal woman who faced a jail sentence for helping her 36-year-old son who also suffered from multiple sclerosis, commit suicide in 2004. At her son's request, Houle prepared for him a lethal mixture of drugs and held a plastic bag over his head until he suffocated. Houle was eventually spared a jail sentence as a result of her emotional state, but her case cast light on the issue of whether those who help their loved ones escape their misery should be viewed as innocents abiding by the last request of their loved ones, or accomplices to murder.

And if family members do not abide by their loved ones wishes to help them die, keeping PAS illegal forces those who take their own lives to do so alone, which supporters of the practice say is cruel and unfair. Indeed, to protect their families and friends from being prosecuted for aiding and abetting a suicide, terminally ill people who choose to end their lives in states where PAS is illegal must do so in private so as not to implicate their loved ones. Supporters of PAS argue this robs people the opportunity of having the people they love with them during the final, last moments of their lives.

All of these arguments have helped physician-assisted suicide remain a legal option for the terminally ill in Oregon for nearly a decade, and in the Netherlands and Switzerland for even longer. Yet the problems, loopholes, and potential for abuse have also been the reasons physician-assisted suicide has been continually defeated by lawmakers and voters in California, Maine, Michigan, Hawaii, Washington, Wisconsin, and Vermont, and in countries around the world. The legality of physician-assisted suicide will continue to be debated as more and more states and countries consider whether it is an appropriate part of their legal code.

Primary Source Quotes*

Should Assisted Suicide Be Legal?

> **"We found no evidence to justify the grave and important concern often expressed about the potential for abuse."**

—Margaret P. Battin et al., "Legal Physician-Assisted Dying in Oregon and the Netherlands: Evidence Concerning the Impact on Patients in 'Vulnerable' Groups," *Journal of Medical Ethics,* vol. 33, no. 10, October 2007, p. 597.

Battin et al., collaborated on a study that that scrutinized Oregon's Death with Dignity Act for evidence of abuse.

> **"Oregon destroys information collected about each patient who chooses to use the law. 'This makes it impossible for any outside researcher to avail themselves on the data. The truth is, we really don't know what's happening in Oregon.'"**

—Marilyn Golden, quoted in Claudia Rowe, "Family Fights for Assisted-Suicide Vote; for a Cancer Patient, It's a Personal Initiative," *Seattle Post-Intelligencer,* July 3, 2008, p. B1.

Golden is a policy analyst with the Disability Rights Education and Defense Fund in Berkeley, California, a group that opposes physician-assisted suicide.

Bracketed quotes indicate conflicting positions.

* Editor's Note: While the definition of a primary source can be narrowly or broadly defined, for the purposes of Compact Research, a primary source consists of: 1) results of original research presented by an organization or researcher; 2) eyewitness accounts of events, personal experience, or work experience; 3) first-person editorials offering pundits' opinions; 4) government officials presenting political plans and/or policies; 5) representatives of organizations presenting testimony or policy.

66 To declare that society or God must give you permission to kill yourself—is to contradict the right to life at its root. If you have a duty to go on living, despite your better judgment, then your life does not belong to you, and you exist by permission, not by right. For these reasons, each individual has the right to decide the hour of his death and to implement that solemn decision as best he can. The choice is his because the life is his. 99

—Thomas A. Bowden, "Assisted Suicide: Moral Right," *Capitalism Magazine,* March 27, 2005. www.capmag.com.

Bowden is a writer for the Ayn Rand Institute, a think tank that promotes the principles of reason, rational self-interest, and individual rights.

66 The Oregon law has nothing to do with the freedom of the individual and everything to do with the power of doctors. If freedom were the concern, we would simply repeal the drug and prescription laws, and recognize each adult's right to buy any kind of drugs. 99

—Sheldon Richman, "The Fraud of Physician-Assisted Suicide," The Future of Freedom Foundation, June 23, 2004. www.fff.org.

Richman is senior fellow at the Future of Freedom Foundation and editor of the *Freeman* magazine.

66 If you personally feel strongly that you don't want what you feel is a loss of dignity, people should have that legal choice. They shouldn't have to sneak around someone's back like in the other 49 states. 99

—Teresa Grove, quoted in Kathie Durbin, "For Assisted Suicide: Teresa Grove," *McClatchy-Tribune Business News,* July 13, 2008.

Grove is a hospice nurse affiliated with the group Compassion and Choices, which sponsored Oregon's Death with Dignity Act.

66 In Oregon, the second consultation typically is sought with a potentially biased physician who lacks either the time or the skill for an in-depth evaluation of the patient and family. 99

—Kathleen M. Foley, "Is Physician-Assisted Suicide Ever Acceptable? It's Never Acceptable," *Family Practice News,* June 1, 2007, p. 11.

Foley is a neurologist who specializes in palliative care and pain management at the Memorial Sloan-Kettering Cancer Center.

66 We want our government to let us to live as we choose. So why do we stand for a government that won't let us die as we choose? 99

—Joan Ryan, "Right to Die Is Necessary Freedom: Fate of Terminally Ill Not Up to Government," *San Francisco Chronicle,* January 9, 2005.

Ryan is a columnist for the *San Francisco Chronicle.*

66 Choices about physician assisted suicide, if they are to have moral significance, must be un-coerced, free choices. And meaningful choices must be available not just to the privileged few but to everyone. A common good lens highlights the stark inequalities in our society that too often constrain, threaten, or even prohibit meaningful free choices for many vulnerable citizens on this issue. 99

—Robert Jones, "The Common Good Argument Against Physician-Assisted Suicide," Catholics in Alliance for the Common Good, February 6, 2008. www.catholicsinalliance.org.

Jones is an author, speaker, and consultant on religion and progressive policies. He is the author of *Liberalism's Troubled Search for Equality: Religion and Cultural Bias in the Oregon Physician-Assisted Suicide Debates.*

66 **Prohibition didn't work with booze or abortions. Regulating euthanasia sounds dreadful, but it may prevent desperate people grievously maiming themselves by going it alone or aided by quacks.** 99

—Robert Lake, "The Case for Legal Euthanasia," *Ottawa Citizen,* July 11, 2008, p. A13.

Lake is a Canadian journalist and a retired psychology professor.

66 **Any licensed physician—including any dermatologist, ophthalmologist, or pathologist—can write lethal prescriptions. It doesn't really take a lot of medical savvy to prescribe a deadly dose.** 99

—Rita L. Marker and Wesley J. Smith, "Dr. Death Rides Again," *Weekly Standard,* vol. 12, no. 35, June 4, 2007.

Marker and Smith are attorneys with the International Task Force on Euthanasia and Assisted Suicide.

66 **Sorry, we say: you are physically incapable of taking your own life (an action decriminalized in [Britain] in 1961), and therefore we must sentence you to whatever physical and mental tortures your mortal biology may send you, for the term of your natural life. If necessary, you must go on and on in unbearable pain, and any doctor who helps you die will be liable to 14 years in prison.** 99

—Boris Johnson, "Assisted Suicide Is Problematic, but Better than Months of Agony," *Telegraph* (London), January 26, 2006.

Johnson is the mayor of London and former editor of the *Spectator* magazine.

66 In all the talk about legally assisted suicide, I do not hear discussed how assisted suicide laws affect those of us who do not want it. What about the temptations such laws impose on those of us who believe that suicide is morally wrong? If I am terminally ill and in pain, why should I have to face the temptation of doing myself in early, when it may pose a risk to my immortal soul? Why should I be forced to suffer this temptation, just so that others, whose beliefs differ from mine, will be allowed their own exit plan? 99

—David A. Shaneyfelt, "Assisted Suicide: Death with Indignity?" *Ventura County Star,* May 6, 2007. www.venturacountystar.com.

Shaneyfelt is an attorney who lives in Ventura, California.

Should Assisted Suicide Be Legal?

- Oregon is the only U.S. state to **have legalized assisted suicide**. Many other states have defeated bills or propositions to legalize it, and seven have laws specifically prohibiting it.

- Assisted suicide has been legal in the **Netherlands** since 2002 and in **Switzerland** since 1941.

- As reported by the *New England Journal of Medicine*, in the Netherlands in 2005, **0.1 percent** of all deaths were the result of assisted suicide.

- The Netherlands reports that about **2 percent** of all deaths there are via assisted suicide (where a physician writes a patient a prescription for lethal medication to self-administer) or euthanasia (where the physician directly administers the lethal medication to a patient).

- According to the Oregon Department of Human Services:
  - Since the DWDA was passed in 1997, **341 patients** have used the law to hasten their own death.
  - Less than **1 percent** of all deaths in Oregon—about **0.15 percent**—occur as a result of physician-assisted suicide.
  - There are an estimated **15.6** assisted suicides for every 10,000 deaths in the state.
  - **46.3 percent** of all assisted suicides have been women.
  - **53.7 percent** of all assisted suicides have been men.

- **1.2 percent** of all assisted suicides have been people between the ages of 18 and 34.
- **2.9 percent** have been between the ages of 35 and 44.
- **9.1 percent** have been between the ages of 45 and 54.
- **21.4 percent** have been between the ages of 55 and 64.
- **27.3 percent** have been between the ages of 65 and 74.
- **28.7 percent** have been between the ages of 75 and 84.
- **9.4 percent** have been 85 or older.
- The median age of people who have elected assisted suicide is **69** years.

Assisted Suicide in the United States

Since Oregon legalized assisted suicide in 1994, 21 other states have attempted to do so. None of these bills have passed, however, and 7 states have actually passed laws specifically prohibiting assisted suicide.

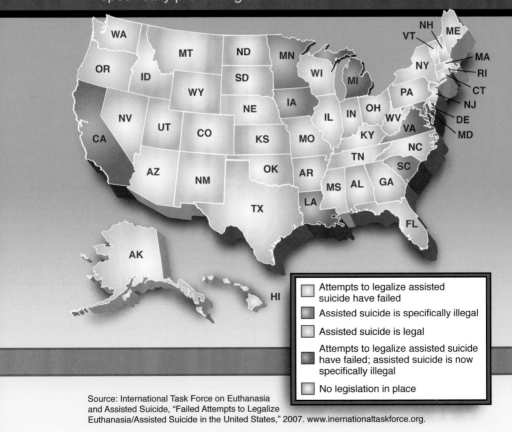

Attempts to legalize assisted suicide have failed

Assisted suicide is specifically illegal

Assisted suicide is legal

Attempts to legalize assisted suicide have failed; assisted suicide is now specifically illegal

No legislation in place

Source: International Task Force on Euthanasia and Assisted Suicide, "Failed Attempts to Legalize Euthanasia/Assisted Suicide in the United States," 2007. www.inernationaltaskforce.org.

Assisted Suicide Around the World

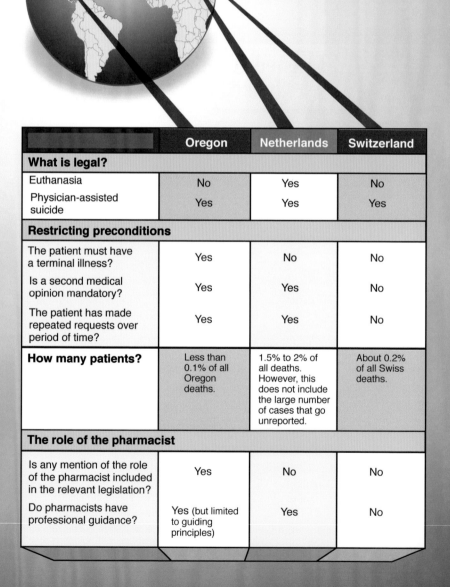

Assisted suicide is legal in just three places in the world, and is regulated differently in each place.

	Oregon	Netherlands	Switzerland
What is legal?			
Euthanasia	No	Yes	No
Physician-assisted suicide	Yes	Yes	Yes
Restricting preconditions			
The patient must have a terminal illness?	Yes	No	No
Is a second medical opinion mandatory?	Yes	Yes	No
The patient has made repeated requests over period of time?	Yes	Yes	No
How many patients?	Less than 0.1% of all Oregon deaths.	1.5% to 2% of all deaths. However, this does not include the large number of cases that go unreported.	About 0.2% of all Swiss deaths.
The role of the pharmacist			
Is any mention of the role of the pharmacist included in the relevant legislation?	Yes	No	No
Do pharmacists have professional guidance?	Yes (but limited to guiding principles)	Yes	No

Source: Royal Pharmaceutical Society of Great Britain, "Pharmacy and Assisted Suicide and Euthanasia: International Experience," 2007. www.rpsgb.org.uk.

- **45.2 percent** of people who have died by assisted suicide were married at the time of their deaths.
- **21.4 percent** were widowed at the time of their deaths.
- **25.2 percent** were divorced at the time of their deaths.
- **8.2 percent** had never been married.

- When asked why they had elected assisted suicide:
  - **100 percent** of participants said because they feared loss of autonomy.
  - **86 percent** said their ability to participate in activities that made life enjoyable had decreased.
  - **86 percent** said to avoid losing their dignity.
  - **33 percent** were concerned about not being able to control their pain.
  - **90 percent** of those who elected assisted suicide in 2007 died at home.

- A 2006 survey by the Pew Research Center found:
  - **55 percent** of Americans believe that killing a spouse who is suffering from a terminally ill disease is justifiable.
  - **36 percent** said they might actually go through with helping a loved one commit suicide.
  - **29 percent** said they could commit the act themselves.

- The 1961 Suicide Act **decriminalized** the act of suicide in Britain, but made helping someone commit suicide punishable by up to 14 years in prison.

- According to a 2008 poll by *ELDR* magazine:
  - **66.3 percent** of Americans favor legalizing assisted suicide.
  - **33.7 percent** oppose it.
  - **68.6 percent** of people younger than 60 favor legalization.
  - **31.4 percent** of people younger than 60 oppose it.
  - **59.1 percent** of people older than 60 favor legalization.
  - **40.9 percent** of people older than 60 oppose it.

- A 2007 AP-Ipsos poll found that:
  - **48 percent** of Americans said assisted suicide should be legal.
  - **44 percent** said it should be illegal.

Americans' Attitudes Toward Legalized Assisted Suicide

National polls consistently reveal that the majority of Americans like the idea of legalized assisted suicide in their state.

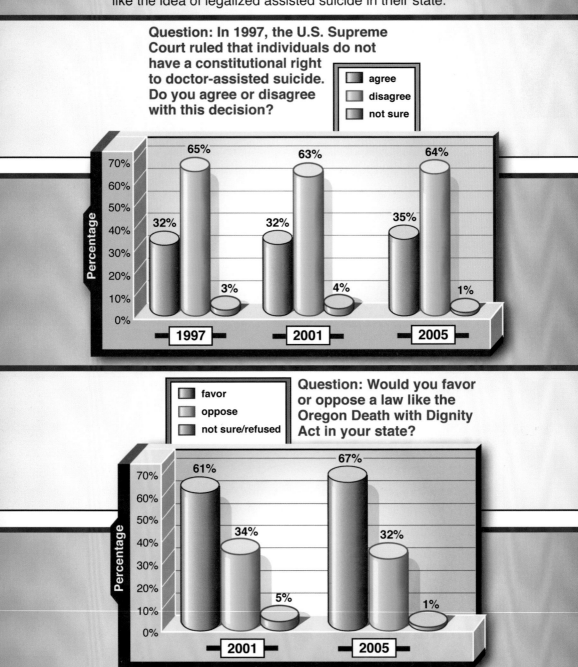

Question: In 1997, the U.S. Supreme Court ruled that individuals do not have a constitutional right to doctor-assisted suicide. Do you agree or disagree with this decision?

- agree
- disagree
- not sure

1997: 32%, 65%, 3%
2001: 32%, 63%, 4%
2005: 35%, 64%, 1%

- favor
- oppose
- not sure/refused

Question: Would you favor or oppose a law like the Oregon Death with Dignity Act in your state?

2001: 61%, 34%, 5%
2005: 67%, 32%, 1%

Source: Harris Poll, "Majorities of U.S. Adults Favor Euthanasia and Physician-Assisted Suicide by More than Two-to-One," #32, April 27, 2005.

Does Assisted Suicide Threaten Vulnerable People?

66 The natural trajectory of assisted suicide advocacy leads to such ever-widening expansions of killable categories: from the terminally ill, to the disabled and chronically ill, to the 'tired of life' elderly, and eventually to the mentally ill. 99

—Wesley J. Smith, attorney with the International Task Force on Euthanasia and Assisted Suicide.

66 As a disabled person, I strongly support the right to die. ... I don't want to linger in a nursing home, wheeled in to a shower room once a week, with others, and be sprayed down. I don't want to be placed every morning in a wheelchair, and parked in the hall for hours at a time. To me, that is not even living, let alone with dignity. 99

—Jolene Noteboom, a California resident who lives with a disability.

A common theme in assisted suicide debates is whether the practice places society on a slippery slope toward eliminating from the population groups of people that are considered to be undesirable, expensive, or otherwise burdensome. Although assisted suicide is supposed to be limited to the terminally ill who have just a few months to live, some worry that once it is accepted, the definition of who is eligible for assisted suicide could be dangerously expanded.

The Threat to the Poor and Uneducated

One vulnerable sector of the population that could be threatened by legalized assisted suicide is the poor and uneducated. Because health care is so expensive, it is feared that lower-income people would make a financial decision to elect PAS to spare their families the cost of paying for their medical treatment. Indeed, in the United States, where health care is expensive and millions of Americans are uninsured, electing physician-assisted suicide is a relatively inexpensive choice. In Oregon, lethal prescriptions reportedly cost between $50 and $150; the cost of long-term care, however, can exceed tens of thousands of dollars. "In a context of such health care inequalities, legalizing PAS puts the working poor who lack insurance at risk of reaching for PAS under financial duress," warns bioethics writer Robert Jones. "In this situation, the coercive power of scarcity pushes the poor toward draconian calculations that those of us with private health insurance do not have to make."[36]

> Some worry that once it is accepted, the definition of who is eligible for assisted suicide could be dangerously expanded.

The fear that legalizing physician-assisted suicide would put financial pressure on the poor to kill themselves rather than seek treatment is reflected in national opinions on legalization. A 2006 poll by the Pew Forum on Religion & Public Life, for example, found that while only about half of the general public opposes legalizing the practice, a whopping 78 percent of minorities with incomes under $50,000 oppose it. In contrast, Jones reports that 61 percent of whites with incomes over $100,000 support legalization. To some, it is telling that poor Americans worry more than wealthy ones about the financial implications of legalization.

No Evidence of Inequality

While such fears are emotionally persuasive, data coming out of Oregon and the Netherlands imply they are unfounded. In a comprehensive 2007 survey published by the *Journal of Medical Ethics*, for example, researchers investigated 10 populations that are typically regarded as vulnerable—people older than 80, women, the uninsured, the poor, the uneducated, the physically disabled, the mentally ill, minors, and racial and ethnic minorities, to name a few—and determined that none had been placed at a disadvantage or were overly represented in the figures of people who had died via physician-assisted suicide. The only people who were overly represented were those who were HIV-positive or suffering from myelodysplastic syndrome (MDS), but neither group was suspected of being victimized.

In fact, the data show that people who elect physician-assisted suicide in Oregon tend to be better educated and wealthier than the general population. For example, according to the Oregon Department of Human Services, the majority of people who have died via physician-assisted suicide since 1997—64.2 percent—have had either some college education, a bachelor's degree, or a graduate-level degree. Just 7.9 percent of PAS deaths were people who had less than a high school degree, and only 27.9 percent were those who stopped their education after high school. These numbers indicate that in Oregon at least, the poor and undereducated are not at risk for unfairly succumbing to physician-assisted suicide.

A Threat to the Mentally Ill

The mentally ill are another group that could potentially be threatened by legalized physician-assisted suicide. This became a pressing concern in 2006, when Switzerland approved new guidelines that made assisted suicide a legal option for the mentally ill. The ruling came after a manic-depressive man petitioned the Swiss high court for his right to die with a doctor's help on the grounds that the European Convention on Human Rights granted him the right to self-determination. The court found the mentally ill man did have this right. However, it did not extend physician-assisted suicide to all people with psychiatric disorders. It exempted, for example, the temporarily depressed or those suffering from mental disorders that are deemed to be curable or improved with treatment. But the court argued that since serious, permanent mental disorders can make life

> **Data show that people who elect physician-assisted suicide in Oregon tend to be better educated and wealthier than the general population.**

seem as unbearable to some people as physically painful, terminal disease did to others, the mentally ill should have the right to end their lives with the help of a physician.

Interestingly, both opponents and supporters of physician-assisted suicide had problems with the new development. For some it was proof that legalized PAS does indeed put society on a slippery slope to sanctioning the death of not just the terminally ill but other groups of people. As Wesley J. Smith puts it, we can "stop pretending that assisted suicide legalization would be just a tiny alteration in public policy restricted only to the terminally ill. That clearly isn't true."[37] Smith and others saw the Swiss decision as proof that widening the terms of physician-assisted suicide threatens large swaths of vulnerable people who should be supported in life rather than encouraged to die.

Another criticism of the Swiss decision was that people who elect physician-assisted suicide are supposed to be mentally competent, capable of making a rational decision about a very serious matter. Yet the very fact of being mentally ill usually casts someone's mental competence into question. Claims that the mentally ill can be both terrifically ill yet also rational and competent were unconvincing to even supporters of assisted suicide. Furthermore, one of the goals of psychiatry is to prevent or curb suicidal impulses in patients. Condoning assisted suicide, therefore, seemed to be a contradiction for the entire profession. Psychiatrist Thomas Schläpfer is one person who believes that giving the mentally ill help committing suicide betrays them when they most need help. "This is not a reasonable decision," said Schläpfer. "It [the desire to commit suicide] is a biased outlook stemming from the disease itself. And since the disease is treatable, it is totally and ethically wrong to offer suicide to these patients."[38]

> "Widening the terms of physician-assisted suicide threatens large swaths of vulnerable people who should be supported in life rather than encouraged to die."

Yet others championed the right of the mentally ill to have access to physician-assisted suicide on the grounds that psychiatric patients should have as much choice to end their suffering as others. The Swiss group Dignitas, which helped bring the case to court, claimed that denying PAS to those suffering from severe depression, schizophrenia, or other mental conditions was a form of discrimination. Ludwig Minelli, the founder of Dignitas, said, "You can't say and you shouldn't say that mentally ill people should not have human rights."[39] For Minelli and others, these human rights include the right to decide when your own life has become unbearable. Jacob M. Appel, a writer who publishes essays on assisted suicide and other bioethics issues, agrees that denying the mentally ill the right to an assisted death is discriminatory. "The taboo against assisted suicide for the mentally ill is a well-meaning yet misplaced response to the long history of mistreatment that those with psychiatric illness have endured in western societies."[40] Appel and others believe that granting physician-assisted suicide to psychiatric patients is a form of empowerment that "maximizes the options available to the mentally ill."[41]

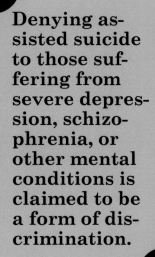

> Denying assisted suicide to those suffering from severe depression, schizophrenia, or other mental conditions is claimed to be a form of discrimination.

The Threat to the Disabled

In addition to the mentally ill and poor, some of the most vocal opponents of assisted suicide are disabled people. They and their families argue the practice puts them in jeopardy by encouraging the death of, rather than the care of, people who are chronically sick, severely handicapped, and otherwise disabled. Even when physician-assisted suicide is limited to the terminally ill, they worry that even starting down the path of legalized killing of one group of people begins a chain reaction that will result in the deaths of disabled people, who have been the victims of such endeavors in the past.

With health-care expenses already at a premium, many in the disabled community envision they could be pressured to end their lives to save their families and communities the cost of their care. Indeed, it costs a lot of money to care for severely disabled people—many need round-the-clock care, live-in nurses, and expensive equipment and medication. Reporter James Ricci explains that disabled people fear the availability of assisted suicide would encourage them to end their lives rather than receive expensive and highly coveted treatments: "Many disability rights activists contend that the increasingly cost-conscious healthcare system, especially health maintenance organizations, inevitably would respond to legalized suicide by withholding expensive care from the disabled and terminally ill until they chose to end their lives."[42]

According to a survey by the UK-based Disability Rights Commission (DRC), people in Great Britain are concerned about this potential for abuse, a main reason it has not yet been legalized there. While 63 percent of the public supports legalizing assisted suicide, more than 80 percent of survey respondents said disabled people need to be protected from potential abuse. This is because evidence exists of disabled people not receiving equal health care even in the absence of physician-assisted suicide: For example, the British Department of Health has found that in general, 85 percent of British women undergo cervical screenings to test for potential problems. In contrast, just 20 percent of women with learning disabilities undergo cervical screenings. Disability rights activists cite this as just one example of how disabled people are systematically disadvantaged by the health-care industry and would be even more so should physician-assisted suicide become legal.

A Life Not Worth Living?

Another threat disabled people see from legalized assisted suicide is that they could potentially be pushed toward death by people who regard their lives as extraordinarily painful or limited and thus not worth living. Professor Rhoda Olkin, who is also a member of the disabled community, has written extensively on the tendency of the nondisabled to view the lives of the disabled as being so insufferable that they would actually be better off dead. She warns, "Medical personnel evaluate the quality of life of persons with disabilities as poor, even when the people themselves evaluate their lives as average or above average."[43] This is confirmed by a study reported in the *Annals of Emergency Medicine,* which found that while 86 percent of quadriplegics rated their quality of life as average or better, only 17 percent of their emergency room doctors, nurses, and technicians rated their quality of life as average or better. Says Olkin, "People without disabilities judge the quality of the lives of people with disabilities more harshly than do the

> " Some of the most vocal opponents of assisted suicide are disabled people. "

people with disabilities themselves. If professionals think that of course the disabled person would want to die, might not these expectations play a disheartening role in someone's decision to seek PAS?"[44]

The expectation that a disabled person would have more reason to want to end his or her life than a nondisabled person is at the heart of the community's opposition to PAS. Claiming it is discriminatory to value one kind of person's life above another's, disabled people point out the hypocrisy involved in thinking that disabled people might have more need or want to end their lives than nondisabled people. Paul K. Longmore, director of the Institute on Disability at San Francisco State University, puts the matter in the following way:

> " **Disabled people are systematically disadvantaged by the health-care industry and would be even more so should physician-assisted suicide become legal.** "

> If a non-disabled person announced their wish to commit suicide, they would get crisis intervention treatment. If a poor Black woman told a judge she could no longer endure racism, sexism, and poverty and wanted judicially sanctioned medical aid to end her life painlessly, she might be offered some minimal support in seeking better housing and a job. She would certainly be refused assistance in killing herself. But when a disabled person declares the same despairing intention, many non-disabled people instantly assume he is acting rationally, because he is confirming their bias that people like him are better off dead.[45]

For all of these reasons, disability rights activists have been the driving force behind defeating assisted suicide bills five times in California, and in other states and nations as well. "The logic of the disability rights movement is easy to understand," says evangelical leader Albert Mohler. "Once a society adopts a *right* to die as a matter of policy, a *duty* to die cannot be far behind. . . . You don't have to be in a wheelchair to see where that leads."[46]

Don't Confuse Disabled with Terminal

But those who fear that the disabled would be lumped into the category of people who should take advantage of legalized assisted suicide are often chided as being overly paranoid. After all, in the United States assisted suicide in Oregon applies solely to terminally ill people with less than six months to live, not the chronically disabled. Protesting assisted suicide on the grounds it could threaten the disabled, in other words, is seen as unnecessary because they are two completely separate conditions: People with chronic but maintainable disabilities have different goals and quality of life than people who have become disabled as a result of an advancing and terminal disease. As disability studies professor Lennard Davis puts it, "Disability activists and scholars have come to see physician-assisted suicide as an assault on the disabled. The fundamental error they've made is that they have equated disability with dying."[47]

> **The expectation that a disabled person would have more reason to want to end his or her life than a non-disabled person is at the heart of the community's opposition to PAS.**

In addition to this distinction, it is often pointed out that as a political group, disabled people tend to and should support liberal issues that invoke the right to privacy and freedom of choice, key related arguments for legalizing physician-assisted suicide. One way in which disabled people have a vested interest in safeguarding the right to privacy is regarding employment—their right to medical privacy, for example, is very important to ensure they are not discriminated against when applying for a job. Making alliances with conservative groups who oppose physician-assisted suicide, it is argued, could therefore backfire and undermine other issues that are important for disabled people to champion. "Every time you encourage one form—any form—of judicial action on the right to privacy," says Davis, "you're weakening it, and we have to be very careful when we choose short-term alliances and strategies. One of the key issues of the right to privacy for people with disabilities is that you don't want your medical records available to employers, insurance companies and so on."[48] In other words, even if they personally never elect physician-assisted suicide, it is argued that disabled people should fight to legalize the practice because it is consistent with other privacy rights that are dear to them.

In Britain, polls of disabled people have evidenced this thinking. A 2004 survey commissioned by the Voluntary Euthanasia Society found a whopping 80 percent of disabled Britons support legalizing assisted suicide for the terminally ill because they believe it would not threaten healthy disabled people and because they believe a disabled person who is terminally ill deserves the right to die with help from a doctor. Furthermore, 77 percent said that prohibiting assisted suicide actually discriminates against disabled people who may be physically unable to end their lives without another person's help. Says one disabled person who participated in a 2005 survey, "Preventing assisted suicide by law prevent[s] only the completely helpless from committing suicide, those who most often are doing the most suffering. It is condemning the most suffering to exist in their misery with no escape. As well as it being an unbelievable cruelty, it is discriminatory."[49] Another disabled person calls attempts to protect disabled people from physician-assisted suicide "patronizing and offensive," arguing, "I don't think anyone has the right to deny physician-assisted death to people who are of sound mind and emotionally stable"[50]—whether they are disabled or not.

> " It is argued that disabled people should fight to legalize the practice because it is consistent with other privacy rights that are dear to them. "

Although Oregon has found no evidence that the disabled, poor, mentally ill, or anyone other than a terminally ill person has been able to die with assistance, members of these groups continue to fight further legalization efforts on the grounds that one day the definition of who should receive assisted suicide could be broadened to include them. Whether physician-assisted suicide indeed threatens vulnerable sectors of society is likely to be an issue in all states and nations that consider legalizing the practice.

Primary Source Quotes*

Does Assisted Suicide Threaten Vulnerable People?

" In a society in which people with disabilities are one of the most disadvantaged minority groups, we do not have the luxury of thinking of PAS as a final act of self-determination. We are a vulnerable population, subject to forced sterilization, ostracization, stigma, and discrimination. . . . It is not paternalistic to think that people with disabilities will be coerced into PAS (or killed without their permission). "

—Rhoda Olkin, "Why I Changed My Mind About Physician-Assisted Suicide,"
Journal of Disability Policy Studies, vol. 16, no. 1, Summer 2005, pp. 70–71.

Olkin is a professor of clinical psychology at the California School of Professional Psychology. She also has a disability.

" The fear is that these laws are going to get rid of people with disabilities—the most fragile, the most helpless—a eugenics argument. But if you look at who's choosing assisted suicide, it turns out to be not that group of people. "

—Lennard Davis, quoted in Mary Johnson, "The Right to Die and Disability Rights: An Interview with Lennard Davis," *Ragged Edge,* October 28, 2005. www.raggededgemagazine.com.

Davis is a professor of disability and human development in the School of Applied Health Sciences at University of Illinois at Chicago.

Bracketed quotes indicate conflicting positions.

* Editor's Note: While the definition of a primary source can be narrowly or broadly defined, for the purposes of Compact Research, a primary source consists of: 1) results of original research presented by an organization or researcher; 2) eyewitness accounts of events, personal experience, or work experience; 3) first-person editorials offering pundits' opinions; 4) government officials presenting political plans and/or policies; 5) representatives of organizations presenting testimony or policy.

Primary Source Quotes

66 **If the values championed by assisted suicide advocates are maximization of autonomy and minimization of suffering—even when they conflict with the extension of life—then it follows that chronically depressed, competent individuals would be ideal candidates for the procedure.** 99

—Jacob M. Appel, "A Suicide Right for the Mentally Ill? A Swiss Case Opens a New Debate," *Hastings Center Report,* vol. 37, no. 3, May/June 2007, p. 22.

Appel is a bioethics writer who regularly contributes to the *Journal of Clinical Ethics,* the *Journal of Law, Medicine & Ethics,* the *Hastings Center Report,* and the *Bulletin of the History of Medicine.*

66 **You don't see poor people demonstrating in the streets or demanding the right to assisted suicide: They are worried about receiving adequate care! . . . The temptation that would be posed by inheritance and life insurance when families pondered whether to support a family member's request for assisted suicide is obvious.** 99

—Wesley J. Smith, "Testimony of Wesley J. Smith Before the California Senate Judiciary Committee," Discovery Institute, June 20, 2006. www.discovery.org.

Smith is an attorney for the International Task Force on Euthanasia and Assisted Suicide and a consultant to the Center for Bioethics and Culture.

66 **Without health insurance terminally ill patients could end up choosing or be pressured into choosing to prematurely end their lives for financial or similar reasons.** 99

—Robert Jones, interviewed in David Masci, "A Progressive Argument Against the Legalization of Physician-Assisted Suicide," Pew Forum on Religion & Public Life, October 3, 2007. http://pewforum.org.

Jones is an author, speaker, and consultant on religion and progressive policies. He is the author of *Liberalism's Troubled Search for Equality: Religion and Cultural Bias in the Oregon Physician-Assisted Suicide Debates.* Masci is a senior research fellow at the Pew Forum on Religion & Public Life.

66 My mother has been tending to me over the past 27 years, feeding me, carrying me to the toilet, and helping me turn around a dozen times during the night. . . . [Legalized assisted suicide] will not only put an end to my pains, but also provide a way out for those suffering the same or more than me. 99

—Li Yan, quoted in Jessie Tao, "Severely Disabled Woman Appeals for Euthanasia Law," *China Daily*, March 15, 2007.

Li is a 28-year-old Chinese woman who suffers from motor neuron disease. She is confined to a wheelchair and can only move her head and a couple of fingers.

66 Many disabled people live their entire lives with such so-called indignities and still find life worth living. But shouldn't each of us decide for ourselves what makes life worth living? Should my standard be forced on you or yours on me? 99

—Joan Ryan, "Right to Die Is Necessary Freedom: Fate of Terminally Ill Not Up to Government," *San Francisco Chronicle*, January 9, 2005.

Ryan is a columnist for the *San Francisco Chronicle*.

66 Even if legislation could protect those with disabilities from the threat of involuntary elimination, how long will it be before the disabled, the elderly, and others requiring extra care begin to wonder if their loved ones would not be better off without them? 99

—Albert Mohler, "A Threat to the Disabled . . . and to Us All," AlbertMohler.com, August 9, 2007. www.albertmohler.com.

Mohler is president of the Southern Baptist Theological Seminary and a leader among American evangelicals.

66 The truth was that David Rivlin might have enjoyed the life he yearned for, but society blocked his efforts, and government policies forced him into a nursing home. Far more than his physical condition, the system created by public policies robbed him of real choices and, in the end, made his life unendurable. 99

—Paul K. Longmore, "Policy, Prejudice, and Reality: Two Case Studies of Physician-Assisted Suicide," *Journal of Disability Policy Studies,* vol. 16, no. 1, Summer 2005, p. 40.

Longmore is a professor of history and the director of the Institute on Disability at San Francisco State University.

66 Undoubtedly there may be some persons who do fit into the 'vulnerable' category, but there are also many of us who are educated, are employed, and have adequate access to the medical, social, and environmental resources that we require. As such, we should be afforded the right to decide for ourselves without being unfairly pathologized. 99

—Karen Hwang, "Attitudes of Persons with Physical Disabilities Toward Physician-Assisted Death: An Exploratory Assessment of the Vulnerability Argument," *Journal of Disability Policy Studies,* vol. 16, no. 1, Summer 2005, p. 16.

Hwang is a postdoctoral candidate at Kessler Medical Rehabilitation Research and Education Corp. She has done extensive research on persons with physical disabilities and is herself a member of the disabled community.

66 The threat of assisted suicide and euthanasia are daily fare for Not Dead Yet. We fight to be heard over the loud voices of players on both sides whose interests should be readily seen as, at best, secondary to the organized voice of those society says are 'better off dead.' So many of us have died too young, never getting a real chance to live. 99

—Diane Coleman, "NDY's Diane Coleman on Million Dollar Baby: Seeing Million Dollar Baby from My Wheelchair," Not Dead Yet, 2005. www.notdeadyet.org.

Coleman is president and founder of Not Dead Yet, a disability rights group that opposes physician-assisted suicide.

66 Is a disabled person vulnerable? Perhaps, but not necessarily. I think it's demeaning to say disabled people don't have the capacity or the right to make the choices others do. How is that respecting the rights of people with disabilities? 99

—Robert Brody, quoted in Joan Ryan, "Right to Die Is Necessary Freedom: Fate of Terminally Ill Not Up to Government," *San Francisco Chronicle,* January 9, 2005.

Brody is a clinical professor of medicine at the University of California, San Francisco School of Medicine and chief of the Pain Consultation Clinic and the ethics committee at San Francisco General Hospital.

66 People who died with a physician's assistance were more likely to be members of groups enjoying comparative social, economic, educational, professional and other privileges. 99

—Margaret P. Battin et al., "Legal Physician-Assisted Dying in Oregon and the Netherlands: Evidence Concerning the Impact on Patients in 'Vulnerable' Groups," *Journal of Medical Ethics,* vol. 33, no. 10, October 2007, p. 597.

Battin et al., collaborated on a study that concluded legalized assisted suicide in Oregon and the Netherlands has not threatened vulnerable groups of people.

66 Proponents [of assisted suicide] tend to be upper middle class or higher; white, well-off, well, and worried. History has taught us that when laws are established by and for controlling people, that the poor are discriminated against. 99

—Kenneth R. Stevens, "The Consequences of Physician-Assisted Suicide Legalization," University of Oregon, McAlister Lounge, October 11, 2005. www.pccef.org.

Stevens is vice president of the Physicians for Compassionate Care Education Foundation.

Does Assisted Suicide Threaten Vulnerable People?

- According to the British group Disability Awareness in Action (DAA), since 1990 more than **16,000 violations** against disabled people have been recorded, **9 percent** of which have threatened their lives.

- A 2008 survey by the disability rights group Disaboom and Kelton Research found that overall, **52 percent** of Americans would choose to die rather than have a severe disability. The survey also found that death over severe disability would be chosen by:
  - **63 percent** of Americans aged 35 to 44;
  - **50 percent** of Americans 55 to 64;
  - **56 percent** of Americans 65 and older;
  - **45 percent** of southerners;
  - **61 percent** of westerners;
  - **57 percent** of college graduates;
  - **30 percent** of people who did not finish high school;
  - **59 percent** of Americans who earn $75,000 a year or more;
  - **45 percent** of Americans who make $25,000 a year or less.

- More than 54 million Americans—**1 in 6 people**—have some form of disability.

- According to the anti-assisted-suicide group Not Dead Yet:
  - **75 percent** of people with spinal cord injuries rate their quality of life as good or excellent.
  - Less than **33 percent** of quadriplegics who use ventilators express dissatisfaction with their lives.

- A 2005 study of disabled people published in the *Journal of Disability Policy Studies* polled two different groups of disabled people—some from the group Carecure, a forum for people who suffer from spinal cord injury, and New Mobility.com, a group whose members suffer from many different disabilities, including cerebral palsy, polio, multiple sclerosis, and spina bifida. The study found:
    - **52 percent** of disabled people from Carecure supported legalizing physician-assisted death, with safeguards.
    - **48 percent** opposed legalization of assisted suicide.
    - **80 percent** of New Mobility.com members supported legalizing physician-assisted suicide.
    - **20 percent** of New Mobility.com members were opposed.

Assisted Suicide and Race

Data from Oregon show that people who elect physician-assisted suicide are overwhelmingly white. Supporters of the Death with Dignity Act use this data to argue against concerns that assisted suicide might be used to encourage the killing of minorities.

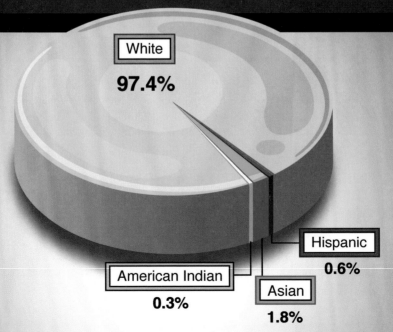

Race of Oregon residents who have elected assisted suicide

White
97.4%

American Indian
0.3%

Asian
1.8%

Hispanic
0.6%

Source: Oregon Department of Human Services, "Death with Dignity Annual Report: Summary for 2007," March 2008. www.oregon.gov.

Americans Who Choose Assisted Suicide Are Well-Educated

Data from Oregon show that 92 percent of people who elect physician-assisted suicide have at least a high school diploma, and more than 60 percent have gone to college, many earning a bachelor's or a graduate degree. Supporters of the Death with Dignity Act use this data to argue against concerns that assisted suicide is issued against the poor.

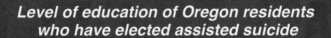

Level of education of Oregon residents who have elected assisted suicide

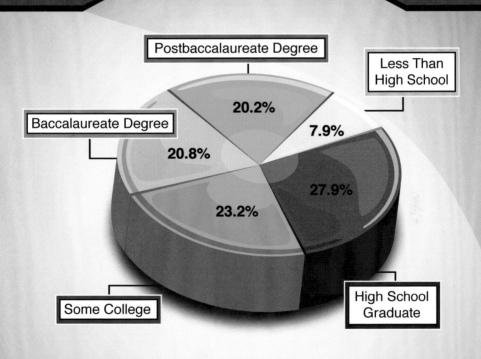

Postbaccalaureate Degree — 20.2%

Less Than High School — 7.9%

Baccalaureate Degree — 20.8%

High School Graduate — 27.9%

Some College — 23.2%

Source: Oregon Department of Human Services, "Death with Dignity Annual Report: Summary for 2007," March 2008. www.oregon.gov.

- Because almost all Dutch citizens are covered by **mandated health insurance**, all patients who have received assisted suicide in the Netherlands have been insured.

Vulnerable Groups Are Not at Risk for Abuse

In 2007 researchers embarked on a comprehensive study to determine whether assisted suicide in Oregon and the Netherlands threatened 10 vulnerable populations. They concluded that none had been placed at a disadvantage or were overly represented in the figures of people who had died via physician-assisted suicide. The only people overly represented were HIV/AIDS patients or patients suffering from myelodysplastic syndrome (MDS), but neither group was suspected of being victimized.

Potentially vulnerable group	Evidence of heightened risk	No evidence of heightened risk
The elderly		X
Women		X
Uninsured people		X
People with AIDS	X	
People with low educational status		X
The poor: people with low socio-economic status		X
Racial and ethnic minorities		X
People with chronic physical or mental disabilities or chronic nonterminal illnesses		X
Minors		X
People with psychiatric illness, including depression and Alzheimer's disease		X

Source: Margaret P. Battin et al., "Legal Physician-Assisted Dying in Oregon and the Netherlands: Evidence Concerning the Impact on Patients in 'Vulnerable' Groups," *Journal of Medical Ethics*, vol. 33, iss. 10, October 2007, p. 596.

- According to the Oregon Department of Human Services, those who elected assisted suicide in Oregon in 2007 all had some form of health insurance:
  - **65 percent** had private insurance;
  - **35 percent** had Medicare or Medicaid.

- Furthermore:
  - **80 percent** of assisted suicides were between 55 and 84 years of age;

- **98 percent** were white;
- **69 percent** had at least some college education;
- **86 percent** suffered from terminal cancer.

Death Without Consent in the Netherlands

A 2007 study published in the *New England Journal of Medicine* found that in the Netherlands in 2001 and 2005, a small yet statistically significant population had their lives ended by a physician without giving their explicit consent. That doctors could use assisted suicide to end the lives of patients without being overtly asked is a concern of those who oppose the practice.

Characteristic	Ending of Life Without Explicit Request by Patient	
	2001	**2005**
Age		
0–64 yr	1.0%	1.0%
65–79 yr	0.4%	0.3%
≥80 yr	0.7%	0.2%
Sex		
Male	0.7%	0.4%
Female	0.7%	0.4%
Type of physician attending		
General practitioner	0.6%	0.2%
Clinical specialist	1.2%	0.7%
Nursing home physician	0.4%	0.3%
Total	**0.7%**	**0.4%**

Source: Agnes van der Heide el al., "End-of-Life Practices in the Netherlands Under the Euthanasia Act," *New England Journal of Medicine*, vol. 356, iss. 19, May 10, 2007, p. 1,962.

What Are the Alternatives to Assisted Suicide?

66 **Once you show that suffering can be relieved without killing, almost nobody chooses killing.** 99

—William Saletan, columnist for *Slate.com*.

66 **I suspect legalizing assisted-suicide on average will prolong life.** 99

—Robert Lake, journalist and former psychology professor.

A ssisted suicide has been proposed as an answer to difficult end-of-life issues that seem to have no other solution. But does legalizing assist-ed death discourage society from investing in better end-of-life and palliative (pain-relieving) care? Does hastening death rob people of time or help them live out their days with peace of mind? These are some of the questions raised when people discuss alternatives to assisted suicide.

Investing in End-of-Life Care

Critics of assisted suicide worry that a consequence of legalizing assisted suicide could be the disintegration of medical institutions that care for people as they near the end of life. In the Netherlands, where both assisted suicide and euthanasia are legal, both end-of-life and palliative care have been reported to be underfunded and deficient compared with countries where such practices are illegal. *Slate* columnist William Saletan explains: "The Dutch experiment didn't improve the care given to people at life's end. Palliative and hospice care got worse, because euthanasia and assisted suicide became easier options."[51]

Evidence of eroding end-of-life care has come out of Oregon as well. For example, Kenneth R. Stevens, vice president of the anti-assisted-suicide group Physicians for Compassionate Care, reports that the state health plan, Oregon Medicaid, covers assisted suicide but does not cover costs for medical treatment of patients who have a less than 5 percent chance of living 5 years. Furthermore, in the first decade of Oregon's Death with Dignity Act, the state stopped paying the pharmaceutical bills of 10,000 poor Oregonians and cut the complete coverage of 75,000 residents. Stevens warns that as assisted suicide becomes an easier, cheaper option than end-of-life care, "assisted suicide may become the 'only choice' for some vulnerable patients."[52]

It is also argued that legalizing assisted suicide not only removes incentives to develop new technologies that can improve a terminally ill patient's quality of life but also reduces society's instinct to seek out cures for disease. If illnesses are increasingly "treated" with assisted suicide, the entire field of medicine could potentially become neglected or lazy. Says one Dutch doctor, "This is my biggest concern in providing [assisted suicide] and setting a norm of euthanasia in medicine: that it will inhibit the development of our learning from patients, because we will solve everything with euthanasia."[53] This is why ultimately, those who oppose physician-assisted suicide view the matter as not taking *away* a right to kill oneself, but *offering* people the right to improved end-of-life and palliative care. As scholar Rhoda Olkin expresses it, "There is an existential absurdity to developing laws and guidelines on the right to die when citizens do not have the right to live."[54]

> A consequence of legalizing assisted suicide could be the disintegration of medical institutions that care for people as they near the end of life.

Helping Doctors Learn Alternatives to PAS

Compounding the problem is that many doctors who participate in PAS are unknowledgeable about end-of-life care, says psychiatrist Herbert Hendlin, author of *Seduced by Death: Doctors, Patients, and Assisted Suicide.* Thus, when they are charged with explaining end-of-life options to their patients, they tend to present care and treatment options superficially and unconvincingly. Indeed, palliative care is an area of medical expertise that not all doctors are trained in. Those who are not tend to offer patients considering assisted suicide more of a light, shallow rundown of their options rather than in-depth palliative care counseling that specialists would approve of. In a review of Oregon's assisted suicide cases, for example, Hendlin found that a formal palliative care consultation was recommended in just 13 percent of cases.

> "If illnesses are increasingly 'treated' with assisted suicide, the entire field of medicine could potentially become neglected or lazy."

Reflecting this tendency, studies show that the less a physician knows about palliative care, the more he or she tends to favor assisted suicide; on the other hand, the more palliative care techniques a doctor knows, the more he or she tends to oppose PAS. Furthermore, a study of Dutch doctors has found that if given the choice, they prefer to be trained in palliative care rather than continue to assist with suicides. "A number of physicians who received the training have publicly expressed their regrets over having previously euthanized patients because they had not known of any viable option,"[55] says Hendlin. Being intimately familiar with and trained in palliative care options, therefore, could be key to showing patients that they have more options than just suffering or suicide.

Finally, it is argued that legalized PAS encourages doctors to give up on patients—a critical part of their duty to care for them until the end. Hendlin shares the story of a Dutch physician who said of a patient who suffered from ALS and was considering physician-assisted suicide: "I can give him the finest wheelchair there is, but in the end it is only a stopgap. He is going to die, and he knows it."[56] Hendlin and others argue that this attitude makes a doctor unable to truly present assisted suicide alternatives to patients, potentially robbing them of years of life.

Creating better palliative care and pain management options could also satisfy a person's need to be in control of the end of his or her life. Repeated studies and polls have shown that most people elect physician-assisted suicide because they want to have control over their death—not because they are actually in unbearable pain but because they fear that one day they will be in unbearable pain. Some doctors recognize the validity of this fear but say it should be met not by offering assisted suicide but by offering better palliative care and pain management. Says Linda Ganzi, director of the geriatric psychiatry fellowship program at Oregon Health and Science University: "Some people want to leave this world in the driver's seat. That's their major goal. And we need to let this goal start driving how they should be cared for—whether they get assisted suicide or not."[57] In other words, Ganzi and others think that patients should be given control not over their deaths, but over their life-prolonging care.

Avoiding Suicidal Impulses

The fear that people will act on suicidal impulses that result from temporary depression rather than from unbearable pain from a terminal illness is another reason people give for supporting alternatives to assisted suicide. "As with other individuals who are suicidal, patients who desire an early death during a serious or terminal illness are usually suffering from a treatable depressive condition,"[58] says Hendlin. Indeed, a key feature of depression is the tendency to suffer from tunnel vision, or short-term perspective, or be unable to competently weigh and see alternatives to their current state. People in this state of mind, therefore, may wrongly see their options as only suicide or suffering and needlessly cut their lives short.

Furthermore, surveys of the terminally ill and disabled have shown that while many people initially react to a disease or disability with severe depression and suicidal impulses, the desire to die can decrease over time. A study published in the *Journal of the American Medical Association*, for example, found that over two months, half of cancer patients studied changed their minds about wanting assisted death. The severely disabled, too, have reported rating their quality of life as good or in some cases better than the nondisabled after enduring an adjustment period of shock and depression. In fact, the organization Not Dead Yet reports that 60 percent of paraplegics claim to feel *more* positively about themselves after having become disabled. Opponents of assisted suicide point to these statistics to show that allowing people who may be temporarily

> " Compounding the problem is that many doctors who participate in assisted suicides are unknowledgeable about end-of-life care. "

depressed to kill themselves is wrong—such people should be offered care, therapy, and treatment rather than help in indulging their suicidal impulses.

Those Who Elect PAS Are Sure of Their Decision

Yet many other studies have confirmed that those who elect physician-assisted suicide are not suffering from temporary, curable depression. Rather, they tend to be resolute in their decision to end their life on their own terms. Data from Oregon indicate that only about 10 percent of terminally ill patients seriously consider assisted suicide. An even fewer number—just 1 percent—end up requesting it from their doctors. Even fewer still actually receive a lethal prescription, and it is estimated that just one-tenth of the 1 percent who request the prescription actually end up taking it. These numbers seem to indicate that PAS is not being elected by large numbers of people jumping on the suicide bandwagon, but only by those who are very resolute in their decision.

> A study of Dutch doctors has found that if given the choice, they prefer to be trained in palliative care rather than continue to assist with suicides.

Further casting doubt on the claim that temporary depression might cause some to hastily elect PAS is the fact that people who receive lethal prescriptions tend to hold on to them for a while before taking them. In Oregon, the average length of time someone holds a prescription before taking it is around 42 to 49 days. Someone who would hold a lethal medication for nearly 2 months' time does not fit the profile of the typical suicidal person, who is more likely to act rashly. In addition, no 911 calls have ever been recorded of people taking their medication and then panicking, wanting to be rescued. According to researcher Karen Hwang, "These figures suggest that most chronically and terminally ill people who request [physician-assisted death] do not appear to be doing so out of transitory depression."[59]

We Shouldn't Let People Give Up Hope

Whether they are depressed or not, one of the most chilling arguments for why alternatives to assisted suicide should be considered come from people who have rejected the option and gone on to live out healthy, meaningful, happy lives. Indeed, success stories abound of people who have either out-lived their diagnoses or powered through the initial shock of becoming disabled, going on to enjoy months, sometimes years, of time that would have been lost had they elected assisted suicide.

Writer Nancy Murray shares the experi-ence of her father, who was diagnosed with esophageal cancer, a painful disease that pre-vented him from swallowing properly. After undergoing a procedure to alleviate his pain, he experienced complications that made it impossible for him to swallow at all. For two months the man persisted this way, losing hope he would ever live a normal life again. "Perhaps if some misguided 'angel of mercy'

> **Depressed people may wrongly see their options as only suicide or suffering and needlessly cut their lives short.**

had appeared at that time with a lethal dose of drugs, offering him the 'right' to 'die with dignity,' my father would be in his grave today," says Mur-ray. "But just one month later, after connecting with the right therapist, he regained his ability to swallow. It was not long before the family celebrated his return to health with a steak dinner at his favorite restaurant."[60]

Robert Woodson, professor of medicine at the University of Wisconsin School of Medicine and Public Health, is another person who has expressed relief that assisted suicide was not available in his state. He recalls a patient of his, a woman in her 40s who suffered from leukemia, a usually fatal bone marrow disease. Although she underwent chemotherapy to treat her illness, tests revealed that she still had high amounts of leukemia in her bone marrow, and hope was lost that she would live much longer. "To my great surprise," remembers Woodson, "she turned up in my clinic several years later. She had been trekking in the Himalayas in Nepal!"[61] Woodson argues that if his patient had asked for assisted suicide, her chart was such that most doctors would have believed she was terminally ill and granted her request. "Doctors regu-larly see the unexpected,"[62] reminds Woodson, and opposes physician-assisted suicide for this reason.

Perhaps the most powerful voice on this topic comes from Richard Radtke, a research professor at the University of Hawaii. Radtke suffers from multiple sclerosis, a condition that has left him paralyzed from the neck down. Despite the fact that he is unable to go to the bathroom, bathe, feed, or dress himself, Radtke has accomplished incredible things and reports loving his life. He has published more than 70 papers; founded the Sea of Dreams Foundation, a disability rights organization; runs a camp for disabled youth; and cares and provides for his wife and nine-year-old daughter, both of whom have only known him as a quadriplegic. Radtke uses his own life as an example of how legalized assisted suicide threatens to snuff out people who have value and promise, even when it seems like they have none. "With the legalization of assisted suicide," he warns, "we will lose a lot of people who can make a difference. We cannot even dream of what those losses might be right now; we would never know."[63]

> **Someone who would hold a lethal medication for nearly two months' time does not fit the profile of the typical suicidal person, who is more likely to act rashly.**

Just Having the Option Can Help

But compelling evidence also exists that the availability of assisted suicide actually improves peoples' quality of life by offering them peace of mind in their last days, weeks, and months. For those terrified of losing control over their bodies, just knowing they have the "exit" of assisted suicide helps them live more enjoyable, comfortable, and in some cases, longer lives. Timothy E. Quill, director of the Center for Palliative Care and Clinical Ethics in New York, explains why the exit aspect of assisted suicide is so beneficial for people facing death:

> Ways can be found to address most physical pain, but suffering is a more complex mixture of physical, psychosocial, existential, and spiritual experiences. Most of the patients who broach the subject of assisted dying want to know that there would be an escape available should their suffering become unbearable, and they will never actually need that assistance if they get excellent palliative care. The possibility of an escape is both critical and reassuring to them.[64]

Evidence that just having access to assisted suicide improves a dying person's outlook comes from Oregon, where many more people discuss and request lethal prescriptions than actually ever end up taking them. In 2007, for example, 85 prescriptions for lethal medications were written to terminally ill patients who satisfied the requirements for assisted suicide. But only 46 people—about half—ended up actually using the medication to end their lives. The rest chose to hold their prescriptions and not use them, some dying of natural causes and others living, taking their illness week by week. "Although many people want to talk about physician-assisted death," says Quill, "few ultimately act."[65] Supporters of legalization argue that just having an "exit" can quiet a dying person's fearful mind so much that they are able to live out their remaining time with a feeling of peace and comfort—and in this sense, are given a better quality of life or even a longer one. As one dying woman who filled a prescription for lethal medication put it: "It is such a relief."[66]

> " Legalized assisted suicide threatens to snuff out people who have value and promise, even when it seems like they have none. "

It remains unclear whether assisted suicide discourages the need to invest in other methods for dealing with difficult end-of-life issues or whether its legalization helps broaden the options available to sick, suffering people. Activists on both sides of the issue will continue to research and debate the topic wherever legalizing assisted suicide is proposed.

What Are the Alternatives to Assisted Suicide?

66 Euthanasia, intended originally for the exceptional case, became an accepted way of dealing with serious or terminal illness in the Netherlands. In the process, palliative care became one of the casualties, while hospice care has lagged behind that of other countries. 99

—Herbert Hendlin, "The Case Against Physician-Assisted Suicide: For the Right to End-of-Life Care," *Psychiatric Times,* vol. 21, no. 2, February 1, 2004. www.psychiatrictimes.com.

Hendlin is professor of psychiatry at New York Medical College and medical director of the American Foundation for Suicide Prevention.

66 Oregon is among the nation's leaders in other markers of good end of life care, including deaths at home, opioid prescribing, hospice enrollment, and public awareness about end of life options. 99

—Timothy E. Quill, "Physician-Assisted Death in Vulnerable Populations: Claims of Increased Risk in These Groups Are Not Supported by Evidence," *British Medical Journal,* vol. 334, September 29, 2007, p. 625.

Quill is professor of medicine, psychiatry, and medical humanities at the University of Rochester (NY), where he directs the Center for Palliative Care and Clinical Ethics.

Bracketed quotes indicate conflicting positions.

* Editor's Note: While the definition of a primary source can be narrowly or broadly defined, for the purposes of Compact Research, a primary source consists of: 1) results of original research presented by an organization or researcher; 2) eyewitness accounts of events, personal experience, or work experience; 3) first-person editorials offering pundits' opinions; 4) government officials presenting political plans and/or policies; 5) representatives of organizations presenting testimony or policy.

> **I would prefer to see us demand better services for the elderly and the dying, services which recognize the needs of the whole individual—medical, physical, spiritual.**

—Roseanna Cunningham, "Care, Not Euthanasia, Is the Answer to the 'Problem' of the Elderly," *Sunday Times* (London), July 20, 2008, p. 21.

Cunningham is a Scottish politician.

> **The way we die in America is often very different from the way we want to die. We can do it better, giving people meaningful time with their families, allowing them to be at home. But most end up prisoners of technology.**

—Steven Pantilat, quoted in Joan Ryan, "Right to Die Is Necessary Freedom: Fate of Terminally Ill Not Up to Government," *San Francisco Chronicle,* January 9, 2005.

Pantilat is director of the Palliative Care Service, University of California at San Francisco.

> **I have a total terror of death. The last thing I'd choose is assisted suicide. . . . But I know that if—when—that time comes, I know that, emotionally, it would really help me if I could have that pill in my pocket—just knowing that it's there would help me get through.**

—Lennard Davis, quoted in Mary Johnson, "The Right to Die and Disability Rights: An Interview with Lennard Davis," *Ragged Edge,* October 28, 2005. www.raggededgemagazine.com.

Davis is a professor of disability and human development in the School of Applied Health Sciences at the University of Illinois in Chicago.

❝Let us not allow the arguments on assisted suicide cloud the major issues of better pain management, palliative care and hospice, and an increased quality of life, which would make this issue a moot point. We need to work toward better life, not toward ways to end it.❞

—Richard Radtke, "A Case Against Physician-Assisted Suicide," *Journal of Disability Policy Studies,* vol. 16, no. 1, Summer 2005, p. 58.

Radtke is the founder of Sea of Dreams Foundation, a disability rights organization. He is also a quadriplegic.

❝How long will it be before doctors start bumping off old women like my grandmother, who say they want to die but don't really mean it?❞

—Tom Utley, "My Grandma Used to Beg for Death. Which Is Why I'm So Uneasy About These 'Assisted Suicide' Campaigners," *Daily Mail* (London), June 13, 2008, p. 14.

Utley is a British journalist who writes for the *Daily Mail,* a London-based newspaper.

❝Knowing assisted suicide is available may give suffering people a sense of control. Their suffering can be terminated when they choose. Often they'll choose to continue listening to life's music if they control the volume.❞

—Robert Lake, "The Case for Legal Euthanasia," *Ottawa Citizen,* July 11, 2008, p. A13.

Lake is a Canadian journalist and retired psychology professor.

66 Physicians' support for euthanasia or assisted suicide drops by two-thirds as they learn more about psychiatric screening and palliative care. Too many don't know about the latest techniques to relieve suffering. Too many don't know that depression is separable from terminal illness and can be cured. 99

—William Saletan, "Alternative Sentence: A Counterproposal to Assisted Suicide," *Slate.com,* March 4, 2005. www.slate.com.

Saletan is Slate.com's national correspondent and author of *Bearing Right: How Conservatives Won the Abortion War.*

66 The evidence from Oregon suggests that access to [physician-assisted death] might actually increase life satisfaction among critically ill persons by assuring them that the option of release is within their control if and when they actually desire it. 99

—Karen Hwang, "Attitudes of Persons with Physical Disabilities Toward Physician-Assisted Death: An Exploratory Assessment of the Vulnerability Argument," *Journal of Disability Policy Studies,* Summer 2005, p. 16.

Hwang is a postdoctoral candidate at Kessler Medical Rehabilitation Research and Education Corp. She has done extensive research on persons with physical disabilities and is herself a member of the disabled community.

66 My purpose and hopes are that people will really understand we do all die, and that dying at an old age is not the same as being very sick when you're 30 or 40 with cancer, and yes, fight if you can. But we are a growing-older generation. And if there's anything I hope to get across to people it's . . . you have to think of it as the ending, just like birth was your beginning. 99

—Julie X, quoted in Katherine Seligman, "Hastening the End," *San Francisco Chronicle,* June 8, 2008.

Julie X was a San Francisco Bay Area resident who in 2008 chose to end her own life after suffering from terminal lung cancer. Because physician-assisted suicide is not legal in California, she was aided by the group Compassion & Choices, who counseled her on how to end her life without a doctor's help.

66 Requests for [assisted suicide] are often motivated by terror of what will happen rather than by current symptoms. Facing uncertainty, some patients fill the vacuum with fantasies and fears. When fears and palliative care needs are addressed, the request for an assisted death usually disappears. 99

—Madelyn Hsiao-Rei Hicks, "Physician-Assisted Suicide: A Review of the Literature Concerning Practical and Clinical Implications for UK Doctors," *BMC Family Practice,* vol. 7, no. 39, June 22, 2006. www.biomedcentral.com.

Hsiao-Rei Hicks is an honorary lecturer at the Institute of Psychiatry, University of London.

66 The hospice movement exists to deliver outstanding care to dying patients and does so. But research suggests that hospice care does not stem the wishes of a notable minority for euthanasia. 99

—A. Chapple, S. Ziebland, A. McPherson, and A. Herxheimer, "What People Close to Death Say About Euthanasia and Assisted Suicide: A Qualitative Study," *Journal of Medical Ethics,* vol. 32, 2007, p. 708.

Chapple, Ziebland, and McPherson work at the Department of Primary Health Care at the University of Oxford. Herxheimer is a writer who specializes in database patient experiences.

66 Being against physician-assisted suicide does not mean that one has to engage in measures that prolong life inappropriately. Many patients opt against more treatment when the chance of major benefit is slim, and it is with this doctor's blessing. 99

—Robert Woodson, testimony regarding Senate Bill 151 before the Wisconsin State Senate Committee on Public Health, Senior Issues, Long Term Care, and Privacy, January 23, 2008. www.cmdahome.org.

Woodson is a professor of medicine at the University of Wisconsin School of Medicine and Public Health.

What Are the Alternatives to Assisted Suicide?

- According to the organization Last Acts, which issues report cards to states for the quality of their end-of-life care:
  - Oregon received a **"D"** grade for its hospice care and an **"E"** grade for its palliative care programs.
  - Only **20 percent** of Oregon hospitals have palliative care programs, and these are used by less than one third of dying residents.

- According to the Oregon Department of Human Services:
  - **88 percent** of people who died via the Death with Dignity Act were enrolled in hospice care.

- According to studies published in the *Lancet* and the *Journal of Clinical Oncology*:
  - General practitioners in the United Kingdom recognize depression in only **39 percent** of their patients.
  - Oncologists recognize mild-to-moderate cases of depression in **33 percent** of cases and severe depression in only **13 percent** of cases.

- As reported in the *Journal of Disability Policy Studies:*
  - **45 percent** of nurses and social workers who had treated hospice patients since 1997 said they had cared for a terminally ill patient who had requested physician-assisted suicide.
  - **30 percent** had cared for a patient who had actually received one.

- In the first 9 years of Oregon's Death with Dignity Act, **60 percent** of people who received prescriptions for lethal medication took it.

- According to the Oregon Department of Human Services:
  - **1 in every 1,000** deaths occurs with physician assistance.
  - **1 in every 50** patients discuss the option of assisted suicide with their doctors.
  - **1 in 6** patients discuss the issue with their families.
  - **54 percent** of people who were written lethal prescriptions ended up actually using the medication to end their lives.
  - **30 percent** died of natural causes.
  - **15 percent** chose to hold on to their prescriptions and wait to use them.

More Lethal Prescriptions Are Written than Are Taken

Each year, almost twice the number of lethal prescriptions are written in Oregon than are actually taken. This is because some people find it comforting just to have the prescription available to them, and end up taking their illness week by week or dying from natural causes.

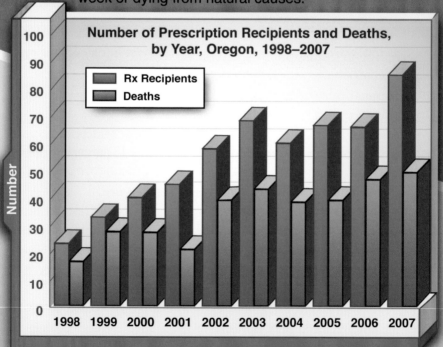

Number of Prescription Recipients and Deaths, by Year, Oregon, 1998–2007

Rx Recipients
Deaths

Source: Oregon Department of Human Services, "Death with Dignity Annual Report: Summary for 2007," March 2008. www.oregon.gov.

Assisted Suicide Candidates Are Largely Dying from Cancer

Data from Oregon show that people who elected physician-assisted suicide between 1997 and 2000 were most often dying from either lung, pancreatic, breast, colon, prostate, and other cancers. In order to receive a lethal prescription, two doctors must determine they have six or less months to live.

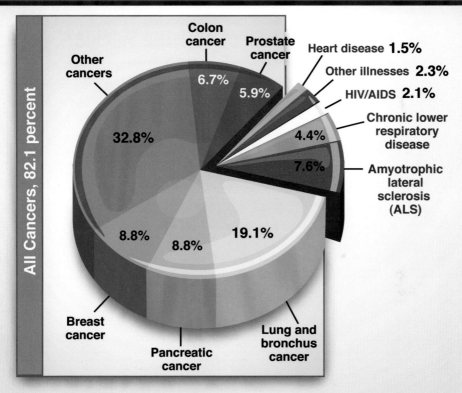

Source: Oregon Department of Human Services, "Death with Dignity Annual Report: Summary for 2007," March 2008. www.oregon.gov.

- According to the Physicians for Compassionate Care Education Foundation:
  - In 2003 and 2004 only **5 percent** of patients who elected physician-assisted suicide in Oregon underwent a mental health consultation to determine if they were depressed.

- In 2004 the doctor who had prescribed a lethal medication for a patient was present at the time of death in only **16 percent** of assisted suicide cases.

- According to the RAND Institute, about **40 percent** of deaths in the United States are preceded by a period of dementia and enfeeblement that lasts up to 10 years. The average life expectancy in the United States is **78** years, compared with **47** years in 1900.

Why Do People Elect Assisted Suicide?

The most commonly given reasons people give for electing assisted suicide include a fear of losing their autonomy, dignity, and control of their bodily functions. The law is supposed to help people escape from unbearable pain, yet interestingly, people rarely elect it because they are actually in pain—more often, they elect it out of a fear of being in unbearable pain in the future.

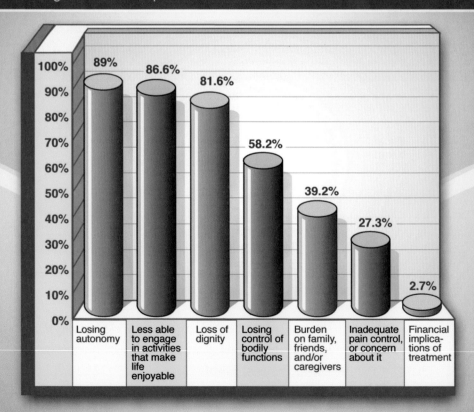

Source: Oregon Department of Human Services "Death with Dignity Annual Report: Summary for 2007," March 2008. www.oregon.gov.

Illicit Drugs in Emergency Room Visits

A survey of more than 1,000 American adults by *ELDR* magazine found that an overwhelming majority would like to receive palliative care (noncurative pain-relief measures) if they find themselves suffering toward the end of their life.

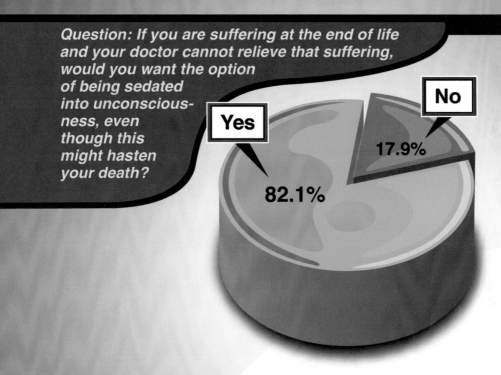

Question: If you are suffering at the end of life and your doctor cannot relieve that suffering, would you want the option of being sedated into unconsciousness, even though this might hasten your death?

Yes
82.1%

No
17.9%

Source: *ELDR*, "Survey Results: The Right to Die," May 14, 2008. www.eldr.com.

- As the baby boomer generation ages, it is expected that more than **13 million** Americans will suffer from Alzheimer's by 2050, most of whom will require many years of expensive, long-term, round-the-clock care.

- None of the three complications among people who ended their lives using the Death with Dignity Act in 2007 resulted from people **changing their minds** at the last minute.

Key People and Advocacy Groups

Diane Coleman: Founder of the organization Not Dead Yet, which opposes assisted suicide on the grounds that it threatens disabled people, Coleman, who is disabled herself, is an active spokesperson for the group.

Compassion & Choices: A national nonprofit organization with 60 chapters that work to improve patients' end-of-life rights, which include access to assisted suicide. The organization was instrumental in getting Oregon's Death with Dignity Act passed in 1994.

Dignitas: Dignitas is a Swiss group based in Zurich that helps people with terminal illness, mental illness, and severe disabilities die.

Kathleen M. Foley: A neurologist who specializes in palliative care and pain management at the Memorial Sloan-Kettering Cancer Center, Foley is considered an authority on assisted suicide. She has written books and testified before Congress on why she believes it should not be legal.

Derek Humphry: Humphry brought assisted suicide into mainstream culture when he wrote the controversial book *Final Exit*, which instructs people how to kill themselves in lieu of having access to legalized assisted suicide. He is currently president of the Euthanasia Research & Guidance Organization (ERGO).

Jack Kevorkian: A Michigan doctor who helped more than 130 people die during the 1990s, Kevorkian was convicted in 1999 of the murder of Thomas Youk and released from prison in 2007.

Ludwig Minelli: A Swiss lawyer, Minelli founded the Swiss assisted suicide group Dignitas in 1998.

Not Dead Yet: An anti-assisted-suicide organization founded by Diane Coleman in 1996, Not Dead Yet opposes efforts to legalize assisted suicide on the grounds that it would threaten disabled people.

Oregon Department of Human Services: This wing of the Oregon government is the main source for data regarding who had elected assisted suicide under that state's Death with Dignity Act.

Physicians for Compassionate Care Education Foundation: Founded by Kenneth R. Stevens, this organization opposes assisted suicide on the grounds that it conflicts with a physician's duty to heal and do no harm.

Diane Pretty: A British woman who suffered from motor neuron disease, Pretty became the focus of efforts to legalize assisted suicide in the United Kingdom in 2002. She petitioned British courts to legalize assisted suicide so she could die with the help of a physician. The courts rejected her appeal, and she died naturally on May 11, 2002.

Peter Rasmussen: A Portland, Oregon, oncologist who specializes in palliative care, Rasmussen has legally assisted in more than a dozen suicides under Oregon's Death with Dignity Act.

Wesley J. Smith: A prolific author on bioethics issues, Smith, an attorney, has written extensively on why he believes assisted suicide and other bioethics issues are immoral and bad policy.

Kenneth R. Stevens: Stevens, a retired radiation oncologist, founded the anti-assisted-suicide group Physicians for Compassionate Care Education Foundation.

Chronology

1828

The earliest American statute to explicitly outlaw assisted suicide is enacted in New York on December 10.

1974

The Society for the Right to Die is founded.

The first American hospice opens in New Haven, Connecticut.

1950

The World Medical Association votes to make its official position that euthanasia be condemned under any and all circumstances.

1961

The act of suicide is decriminalized in Great Britain, but the maximum sentence for assisting a suicide is established at 14 years.

1987

The California State Bar Conference becomes the first public body to approve of physician-assisted suicide.

1950   1960   1970   1980   1990

1972

The U.S. Senate Special Commission on Aging holds the first national hearings on dying with dignity and assisted suicide.

1988

The Unitarian Universalist Association of Congregations passes a national resolution favoring aid in dying for the terminally ill. The decision makes it the first religious body to do so.

1952

The Euthanasia Society of America petitions the United Nations Human Rights Commission to declare that people dying from an incurable disease have the right to die. The United Nations does not grant the request.

1990

Physician Jack Kevorkian assists Janet Adkins, a member of the pro-assisted-suicide Hemlock Society, in committing suicide in Michigan. Adkins's death is the first of 130 suicides in which Kevorkian will ultimately assist.

1946

The Committee of 1776 Physicians for Legalizing Voluntary Euthanasia in New York State is founded.

1991

The state of Washington introduces ballot Initiative 119 to legalize physician-assisted suicide, but voters defeat it.

1992
The state of California introduces Proposition 161 to legalize physician-assisted suicide, but voters defeat it by a margin of 54-46 percent.

1998
A video of Jack Kevorkian administering a lethal injection to Thomas Youk, a Lou Gehrig's disease sufferer, is shown on *60 Minutes*.

Michigan introduces Proposal B to legalize physician-assisted suicide. The proposal is defeated by a huge margin of 71-29 percent.

2000
Maine introduces a ballot initiative for a Death with Dignity Act. It is defeated by a narrow margin of 51-49 percent.

2001
The Netherlands officially legalizes euthanasia and assisted suicide.

2006
The Supreme Court, in a 6-3 opinion in *Gonzales v. Oregon*, upholds Oregon's Death with Dignity Act.

2007
After serving eight years, Kevorkian is released from prison on June 1.

1995   **1998**   **2001**   **2004**   **2007**

1997
Oregonians vote 60 to 40 percent in favor of retaining the Death with Dignity Act, and it begins to be used.

2003
Attorney General John Ashcroft asks the 9th Circuit Court of Appeals to overturn the Oregon Death with Dignity Act on the grounds that it does not serve a legitimate medical purpose.

1999
A Michigan court convicts Kevorkian for Youk's murder and sentences him to 10 to25 years in prison.

2008
Backers of Initiative 1000, the Washington Death with Dignity Act, submit 320,000 signatures to the secretary of state to put the measure on the November 2008 ballot.

1994
The Oregon Death with Dignity Act is passed, becoming the first law in American history permitting physician-assisted suicide. A U.S. District Court judge prevents it from going into effect, however.

Related Organizations

The American Life League (ALL)

PO Box 1350

Stafford, VA 22555

phone: (540) 659-4171

e-mail: info@all.org

Web site: www.all.org

ALL believes that human life is sacred. As such, it opposes assisted suicide and works to educate Americans on its position regarding euthanasia and other bioethics issues. It publishes the bimonthly pro-life magazine *Celebrate Life* and distributes various publications that present its position.

American Society of Law, Medicine, and Ethics

765 Commonwealth Ave., Suite 1634

Boston, MA 02215

phone: (617) 262-4990

e-mail: info@aslme.org

Web site: www.aslme.org

The society's members include physicians, attorneys, health-care administrators, and others interested in the relationship between law, medicine, and ethics. The organization has an information clearinghouse and a library, and it acts as a forum for discussion of many bioethics issues, including assisted suicide.

Autonomy, Inc.

14 Strawberry Hill Lane

Danvers, MA 01923

phone: (617) 320-0506

e-mail: paspiers@autonomynow.org

Web site: www.autonomynow.org

Autonomy, Inc. represents the interests of disabled people who want legal, safe access to physician-assisted suicide and in matters of pain management, hospice care, and legalizing PAS. The organization also supports Oregon's Death with Dignity Act and has filed briefs in major assisted suicide cases.

Compassion & Choices

PO Box 101810

Denver, CO 80250-1810

phone: (800) 247-7421

Web site: www.compassionandchoices.org

Compassion & Choices believes that terminally ill, mentally competent adults should have the right to choose to die without pain and suffering. The organization has been a key player in Oregon's Death with Dignity Act and has worked to counsel people living both in and outside of Oregon on end-of-life options.

Dignity in Dying

181 Oxford St.

London W1D 2JT

England

phone: 0870-777-7868

e-mail: info@dignityindying.org.uk

Web site: www.dignityindying.org.uk

Formerly the Voluntary Euthanasia Society, this British group seeks to legalize physician-assisted suicide in the United Kingdom. Their stated mission is to secure the right for people to be able to die with dignity at the end of their lives. Their Web site offers information about the issue as well as compelling personal stories.

Dying with Dignity

55 Eglinton Ave. East, Suite 802

Toronto, ON M4P 1G8

Canada

phone: (800) 495-6156

e-mail: info@dyingwithdignity.ca

Web site: www.dyingwithdignity.ca

Dying with Dignity seeks to legalize physician-assisted suicide in Canada. It participates in educational and counseling efforts for individuals faced with making important end-of-life decisions. The group also seeks to improve hospice and palliative care services and is active in promoting legislative change that will ensure people experience the best possible end-of-life options, including physician aid-in-dying if they so choose.

Euthanasia Prevention Coalition

Box 25033

London, Ontario N6C 6A8

Canada

phone: (877) 439-3348

e-mail: info@epcc.ca

Web site: www.epcc.ca

This Canadian group's mission is to create social barriers against physician-assisted suicide and euthanasia. The group offers information packages for schools, churches, politicians, hospice and palliative care groups, and the general public. They have also produced a DVD explaining why they believe euthanasia and physician-assisted suicide threaten the disabled and other vulnerable groups of people.

Euthanasia World Directory

24829 Norris Lane

Junction City, OR 97448-9559

phone: (541) 998-1873

e-mail: ergo@efn.org

Web site: www.finalexit.org

The Euthanasia World Directory is the doorway to several pro-assisted-suicide outfits, the most famous of which is the Euthanasia Research &

Guidance Organization (ERGO). ERGO is a nonprofit organization founded to educate patients, physicians, and the general public about euthanasia and physician-assisted suicide. In addition to providing books, pamphlets, essays, and other pieces of research, ERGO conducts opinion polls on the issues, drafts assisted suicide guidelines for physicians and patients, and counsels dying patients.

Human Life International (HLI)

4 Family Life Lane

Front Royal, VA 22630

phone: (800) 549-5433

e-mail: hli@hli.org

Web site: www.hli.org

HLI opposes assisted suicide on the grounds that it is morally unacceptable. It takes this position on other bioethics issues and is committed to defending the rights of the unborn, the disabled, and other groups it believes are threatened by legalized assisted suicide.

International Anti-Euthanasia Task Force (IAETF)

PO Box 760

Steubenville, OH 43952

phone: (740) 282-3810

e-mail: info@iaetf.org

Web site: www.iaetf.org

The IAETF works to prevent assisted suicide from becoming legal in both the United States and abroad. Its Web site and publications address the issues of euthanasia, assisted suicide, advance directives, assisted suicide proposals, "right-to-die" assisted suicide in Oregon cases, euthanasia practices in the Netherlands, disability rights, pain control, and more.

National Hospice and Palliative Care Organization

1700 Diagonal Rd., Suite 625

Alexandria, VA 22314

phone: (703) 837-1500

e-mail: nhpco_info@nhpco.org

Web site: www.nho.org

The National Hospice and Palliative Care Organization opposes assisted suicide and works to educate the public about the benefits of hospice care for the terminally ill and their families. It supports the idea that with the proper care and pain medication, the terminally ill can live out their lives comfortably and in the company of their families.

National Right to Life Committee (NRLC)

512 10th St. NW

Washington, DC 20004

phone: (202) 626-8800

e-mail: NRLC@nrlc.org

Web site: www.nrlc.org

The NRLC is a very active and vocal group that opposes assisted suicide and other bioethics issues such as euthanasia and abortion. The committee publishes the newsletter *NRL News* and frequently commissions editorials and other articles that are written from an anti-assisted-suicide perspective.

The Right to Die Society of Canada

145 Macdonell Ave.

Toronto, ON M6R 2A4

Canada

phone: (416) 535-0690

e-mail: contact-rtd@righttodie.ca

Web site: www.righttodie.ca

This Canadian organization supports the right of any mature individual who is chronically or terminally ill to choose the time, place, and means of his or her death. Its publications include *Free to Go*, a publication that features pro-assisted-suicide articles several times throughout the year.

For Further Research

Books

Kathleen M. Foley and Herbert Hendin, eds., *The Case Against Assisted Suicide: For the Right to End-of-Life Care.* Baltimore, MD: Johns Hopkins University Press, 2004.

Neil M. Gorsuch, *The Future of Assisted Suicide and Euthanasia.* Princeton, NJ: Princeton University Press, 2006.

Derek Humphry, *Final Exit: The Practicalities of Self-Deliverance and Assisted Suicide for the Dying.* New York: Delta, 2002.

Robert P. Jones, *Liberalism's Troubled Search for Equality: Religion and Cultural Bias in the Oregon Physician-Assisted Suicide Debates.* Notre Dame, IN: University of Notre Dame Press, 2007.

Rachel M. MacNair and Stephen Zunes, eds., *Consistently Opposing Killing: From Abortion to Assisted Suicide, the Death Penalty, and War.* New York: Praeger, 2008.

John B. Mitchell, *Understanding Assisted Suicide: Nine Issues to Consider.* Ann Arbor, MI: University of Michigan Press, 2007.

Periodicals

American Medical Association, "Physician Assisted Suicide," Policy H-140.952, 2007. www.ama-assn.org.

Jacob M. Appel, "A Suicide Right for the Mentally Ill? A Swiss Case Opens a New Debate," *Hastings Center Report*, vol. 37, no. 3, May/June 2007.

Margaret P. Battin et al., "Legal Physician-Assisted Dying in Oregon and the Netherlands: Evidence Concerning the Impact on Patients in 'Vulnerable' Groups," *Journal of Medical Ethics*, vol. 33, no. 10, October 2007.

Thomas A. Bowden, "Assisted Suicide: A Moral Right," *Capitalism Magazine*, March 27, 2005. www.capmag.com.

Eric Cohen and Leon R. Kass, "'Cast Me Not Off in Old Age,'" *Commentary*, January 2006.

Diane Coleman, "NDY's Diane Coleman on Million Dollar Baby: Seeing Million Dollar Baby from My Wheelchair," Not Dead Yet, 2005. www.notdeadyet.org.

Roseanna Cunningham, "Care, Not Euthanasia, Is the Answer to the 'Problem' of the Elderly," *Sunday Times* (London), July 20, 2008.

Len Doyal and Lesley Doyal, "Why Active Euthanasia and Physician-Assisted Suicide Should Be Legalized," *British Medical Journal*, vol. 323, November 10, 2001.

Kathie Durbin, "For Assisted Suicide: Teresa Grove," *McClatchy-Tribune Business News*, July 13, 2008.

Kathleen M. Foley, "Is Physician-Assisted Suicide Ever Acceptable? It's Never Acceptable," *Family Practice News*, June 1, 2007.

Michael B. Gill, "A Moral Defense of Oregon's Physician-Assisted Suicide Law," *Mortality*, vol. 10, no. 1, February 2005. www.u.arizona.edu.

Beth Hale, "Will My Husband Face Jail if He Helps Me Die? MS Sufferer Wins the Right to Have the Law Clarified," *Daily Mail* (London), June 12, 2008.

Herbert Hendlin, "The Case Against Physician-Assisted Suicide: For the Right to End-of-Life Care," *Psychiatric Times*, vol. 21, no. 2, February 1, 2004. www.psychiatrictimes.com.

Madelyn Hsiao-Rei Hicks, "Physician-Assisted Suicide: A Review of the Literature Concerning Practical and Clinical Implications for UK Doctors," *BMC Family Practice*, vol. 7, no. 39, June 22, 2006. www.biomedcentral.com.

Karen Hwang, "Attitudes of Persons with Physical Disabilities Toward Physician-Assisted Death: An Exploratory Assessment of the Vulnerability Argument," *Journal of Disability Policy Studies*, vol. 16, no. 1, Summer 2005.

Boris Johnson, "Assisted Suicide Is Problematic, but Better than Months of Agony," *Telegraph* (London), January 26, 2006.

Mary Johnson, "The Right to Die and Disability Rights: An Interview with Lennard Davis," *Ragged Edge*, October 28, 2005. www.raggededgemagazine.com.

Robert Jones, "The Common Good Argument Against Physician-Assisted Suicide," Catholics in Alliance for the Common Good, February 6, 2008. www.catholicsinalliance.org.

Robert Lake, "The Case for Legal Euthanasia," *Ottawa Citizen*, July 11, 2008.

Paul K. Longmore, "Policy, Prejudice, and Reality: Two Case Studies of Physician-Assisted Suicide," *Journal of Disability Policy Studies*, vol. 16, no. 1, Summer 2005.

Jane Saladof MacNeil, "Oregon Experience Sheds Light on End-of-Life Care," *Internal Medicine News*, February 1, 2006.

Rita L. Marker and Wesley J. Smith, "Dr. Death Rides Again," *Weekly Standard*, vol. 12, no. 35, June 4, 2007.

David Masci, "A Progressive Argument Against the Legalization of Physician-Assisted Suicide," Pew Forum on Religion & Public Life, October 3, 2007. http://pewforum.org.

Herb Matthews, "Law Allowed a Dignified Death," *Register-Guard* (Oregon), October 15, 2005. http://rgweb.registerguard.com.

Albert Mohler, "A Threat to the Disabled . . . and to Us All," Albert Mohler.com, August 9, 2007. www.albertmohler.com.

Nancy Murray, "Terminally Ill Need Love, Reassurance," *Tri-City Herald* (Pasco, WA), July 20, 2008.

Rhoda Olkin, "Why I Changed My Mind About Physician-Assisted Suicide," *Journal of Disability Policy Studies*, vol. 16, no. 1, Summer 2005.

Timothy E. Quill, "Physician-Assisted Death in Vulnerable Populations: Claims of Increased Risk in These Groups Are Not Supported by Evidence," *British Medical Journal*, vol. 334, September 29, 2007.

Richard Radtke, "A Case Against Physician-Assisted Suicide," *Journal of Disability Policy Studies*, vol. 16, no. 1, Summer 2005.

James Ricci, "Assisted Suicide Attacked from an Unlikely Front— Disability Rights Groups, Typically Supportive of Individual Liberty, Have Helped Defeat Bills Out of Fear That HMOs Would See a Chance to Cut Care," *Los Angeles Times*, August 6, 2007. http://articles.latimes.com.

Sheldon Richman, "The Fraud of Physician-Assisted Suicide," Future of Freedom Foundation, June 23, 2004. www.fff.org.

Claudia Rowe, "Family Fights for Assisted-Suicide Vote; for a Cancer Patient, It's a Personal Initiative," *Seattle Post-Intelligencer*, July 3, 2008.

Joan Ryan, "Right to Die Is Necessary Freedom: Fate of Terminally Ill Not Up to Government," *San Francisco Chronicle*, January 9, 2005.

William Saletan, "Alternative Sentence: A Counterproposal to Assisted Suicide," *Slate.com*, March 4, 2005. www.slate.com.

Katherine Seligman, "Hastening the End," *San Francisco Chronicle*, June 8, 2008.

David A. Shaneyfelt, "Assisted Suicide: Death with Indignity?" *Ventura County Star*, May 6, 2007. www.venturacountystar.com.

Peter Singer, "Law Reform, or DIY Suicide," *Free Inquiry*, February/March 2005.

Wesley J. Smith, "First, Do Harm . . . a Betrayal of the Hospice Movement," *Weekly Standard*, vol. 12, no. 26, March 19, 2007.

Daniel Sokol, "The Ethics of Assisted Suicide," British Broadcasting Company, May 11, 2006.

Margaret Somerville, "The Case Against Euthanasia; It's Impossible Not to Be Moved by a Plea to End Someone's Suffering—but the Arguments Against Assisted Suicide Are Ultimately More Compelling," *Ottawa Citizen*, June 27, 2008.

Wesley Sowers, "Physician Aid in Dying and the Role of Psychiatry," *Psychiatric Times*, January 1, 2004.

Kenneth R. Stevens Jr., "Emotional and Psychological Effects of Physician-Assisted Suicide and Euthanasia on Participating Physicians," *Issues in Law & Medicine*, vol. 21, no. 3, Spring 2006.

Jessie Tao, "Severely Disabled Woman Appeals for Euthanasia Law," *China Daily*, March 15, 2007.

Tom Utley, "My Grandma Used to Beg for Death. Which Is Why I'm So Uneasy About These 'Assisted Suicide' Campaigners," *Daily Mail* (London), June 13, 2008.

Wake Forest University Baptist Medical Center, "Research Suggests Doctor-Assisted Suicide Wouldn't Undermine Patient Trust," December 6, 2005. www1.wfubmc.edu.

Web Sites

ADAPT (www.adapt.org).

Dignitas (www.dignitas.ch).

The Hemlock Society (www.hemlock.org).

Not Dead Yet (www.notdeadyet.org).

Oregon Department of Human Services Death with Dignity Act (www.oregon.gov/DHS/ph/pas/).

Physicians for Compassionate Care Education Foundation (www.pccef.org).

Source Notes

Overview

1. Quoted in Mary Johnson, "The Right to Die and Disability Rights: An Interview with Lennard Davis," *Ragged Edge*, October 28, 2005. www.raggededgemagazine.com.
2. Robert Lake, "The Case for Legal Euthanasia," *Ottawa Citizen*, July 11, 2008, p. A13.
3. Herbert Hendlin, "The Case Against Physician-Assisted Suicide: For the Right to End-of-Life Care," *Psychiatric Times*, vol. 21, no. 2, February 1, 2004. www.psychiatrictimes.com.
4. Bernard Law, testimony, "Hearing on Ethical, Legal, and Social Issues in Assisted Suicide," House Commerce Subcommittee on Health and Environment, March 6, 1997. www.usccb.org.
5. Kevin Yuill, "The 'Right to Die?' No Thanks," *Spiked*, May 19, 2006. www.spiked-online.com.
6. Yuill, "The 'Right to Die?' No Thanks."

Is Assisted Suicide Moral?

7. Lake, "The Case for Legal Euthanasia," p. A13.
8. Wesley Sowers, "Physician Aid in Dying and the Role of Psychiatry," *Psychiatric Times*, January 1, 2004.
9. Quoted in National Institutes of Health: National Library of Medicine, History of Medicine Division, "Greek Medicine." www.nlm.nih.gov.
10. Physicians for Compassionate Care Education Foundation, "March Posting," March 20, 2008. www.pccef.org.
11. Kenneth R. Stevens Jr., "Emotional and Psychological Effects of Physician-Assisted Suicide and Euthanasia on Participating Physicians," *Issues in Law &*
Medicine, vol. 21, no. 3, Spring 2006, pp. 187–201.
12. American Medical Association, "Physician Assisted Suicide," Policy H-140.952. www.ama-assn.org.
13. Michael B. Gill, "A Moral Defense of Oregon's Physician-Assisted Suicide Law," *Mortality*, vol. 10, no. 1, February 2005, p. 61. www.u.arizona.edu.
14. Quoted in National Institutes of Health: National Library of Medicine, History of Medicine Division, "Greek Medicine."
15. Daniel Sokol, "The Ethics of Assisted Suicide," British Broadcasting Company, May 11, 2006.
16. Quoted in Wake Forest University Baptist Medical Center, "Research Suggests Doctor-Assisted Suicide Wouldn't Undermine Patient Trust," December 6, 2005. www1.wfubmc.edu.
17. Herb Matthews, "Law Allowed a Dignified Death," *Register-Guard* (Oregon), October 15, 2005. http://rgweb.registerguard.com.
18. Yomery Santana, "If I Only Knew . . . ," Death with Dignity National Center, June 27, 2005. www.deathwithdignity.org.
19. Wesley J. Smith, "First, Do Harm . . . A Betrayal of the Hospice Movement," *Weekly Standard*, vol. 12, no. 26, March 19, 2007.
20. Margaret Somerville, "The Case Against Euthanasia; It's Impossible Not to Be Moved by a Plea to End Someone's Suffering—but the Arguments Against Assisted Suicide Are Ultimately More Compelling," *Ottawa Citizen*, June 27, 2008, p. A15.

21. Lake, "The Case for Legal Euthanasia," p. A13.

Should Assisted Suicide Be Legal?

22. Kathleen M. Foley, "Is Physician-Assisted Suicide Ever Acceptable? It's Never Acceptable," *Family Practice News*, June 1, 2007, p. 11.
23. Rita L. Marker and Wesley J. Smith, "Dr. Death Rides Again," *Weekly Standard*, vol. 12, no. 35, June 4, 2007.
24. Rhoda Olkin, "Why I Changed My Mind About Physician-Assisted Suicide," *Journal of Disability Policy Studies*, vol. 16, no. 1, Summer 2005, p. 69.
25. Thomas A. Bowden, "Assisted Suicide: A Moral Right," *Capitalism Magazine*, March 27, 2005. www.capmag.com.
26. Bowden, "Assisted Suicide: A Moral Right."
27. Nancy Murray, "Terminally Ill Need Love, Reassurance," *Tri-City Herald* (Pasco, WA), July 20, 2008, p. F1.
28. Len Doyal and Lesley Doyal, "Why Active Euthanasia and Physician Assisted Suicide Should Be Legalized," *British Medical Journal*, vol. 323, November 10, 2001, p. 1,079.
29. Joan Ryan, "Right to Die Is Necessary Freedom: Fate of Terminally Ill Not Up to Government," *San Francisco Chronicle*, January 9, 2005.
30. Boris Johnson, "Assisted Suicide Is Problematic, but Better than Months of Agony," *Telegraph* (London), January 26, 2006.
31. Quoted in Smith, "First, Do Harm."
32. Smith, "First, Do Harm."
33. Diane, "Diane's Story," Compassion and Choices.org, 2005. www.compassion andchoices.org
34. Sowers, "Physician Aid in Dying and the Role of Psychiatry."
35. Quoted in Beth Hale, "Will My Husband Face Jail If He Helps Me Die? MS Sufferer Wins the Right to Have the Law Clarified," *Daily Mail* (London), June 12, 2008, p. 19.

Does Assisted Suicide Threaten Vulnerable People?

36. Robert Jones, "The Common Good Argument Against Physician-Assisted Suicide," Catholics in Alliance for the Common Good, February 6, 2008. www.catholicsinalliance.org.
37. Wesley J. Smith, "Death on Demand: The Assisted-Suicide Movement Sheds Its Fig Leaf," *Weekly Standard*, July 3, 2007.
38. Quoted in Isobel Johnson, "Switzerland—Death Tourism Capital?" *Swiss Info.ch*, September 14, 2003.
39. Quoted in CBS News.com, "Switzerland's Suicide Tourists: *60 Minutes II* Accompanies German Patient to his Death," July 23, 2003. www.cbsnews.com.
40. Jacob M. Appel, "A Suicide Right for the Mentally Ill? A Swiss Case Opens a New Debate," *Hastings Center Report*, vol. 37, no. 3, May/June 2007, p. 22.
41. Appel, "A Suicide Right for the Mentally Ill?" p. 22.
42. James Ricci, "Assisted Suicide Attacked from an Unlikely Front—Disability Rights Groups, Typically Supportive of Individual Liberty, Have Helped Defeat Bills Out of Fear That HMOs Would See a Chance to Cut Care," *Los Angeles Times*, August 6, 2007, p. B1. http://articles.latimes.com.
43. Olkin, "Why I Changed My Mind About Physician-Assited Suicide," p. 69.
44. Olkin, "Why I Changed My Mind About Physician-Assited Suicide," p. 70.
45. Paul K. Longmore, "Policy, Prejudice, and Reality: Two Case Studies of Physician-Assisted Suicide," *Journal of Disability Policy Studies*, vol. 16, no. 1, Summer 2005, p. 40.
46. Albert Mohler, "A Threat to the Disabled . . . and to Us All," AlbertMohler.com, August 9, 2007. www.albert mohler.com.

47. Quoted in Mary Johnson, "The Right to Die and Disability Rights."

48. Quoted in Mary Johnson, "The Right to Die and Disability Rights."

49. Quoted in Karen Hwang, "Attitudes of Persons with Physical Disabilities Toward Physician-Assisted Death: An Exploratory Assessment of the Vulnerability Argument," *Journal of Disability Policy Studies*, vol. 16, no. 1, Summer 2005, p. 18.

50. Quoted in Hwang, "Attitudes of Persons with Physical Disabilities Toward Physician-Assisted Death," p. 18.

What Are the Alternatives to Assisted Suicide?

51. William Saletan, "Alternative Sentence: A Counterproposal to Assisted Suicide," *Slate.com*, March 4, 2005. www.slate.com.

52. Kenneth R. Stevens, "The Consequences of Physician-Assisted Suicide Legalization," University of Oregon, McAlister Lounge, October 11, 2005. www.pccef.org.

53. Quoted in Select Committee on the Assisted Dying for the Terminally Ill Bill, *Assisted Dying for the Terminally Ill Bill HL*, vol. 2, *Evidence*. London: Stationery Office, April 4, 2005.

54. Olkin, "Why I Changed My Mind About Physician-Assisted Suicide," p. 69.

55. Hendlin, "The Case Against Physician-Assisted Suicide."

56. Quoted in Hendlin, "The Case Against Physician-Assisted Suicide."

57. Quoted in Jane Saladof MacNeil, "Oregon Experience Sheds Light on End-of-Life Care," *Internal Medicine News*, February 1, 2006.

58. Hendlin, "The Case Against Physician-Assisted Suicide."

59. Hwang, "Attitudes of Persons with Physical Disabilities Toward Physician-Assisted Death," p. 16.

60. Murray, "Terminally Ill Need Love, Reassurance," p. F1.

61. Robert Woodson, testimony regarding Senate Bill 151 before the Wisconsin State Senate Committee on Public Health, Senior Issues, Long Term Care and Privacy, January 23, 2008. www.cmdahome.org.

62. Woodson, testimony regarding Senate Bill 151.

63. Richard Radtke, "A Case Against Physician-Assisted Suicide," *Journal of Disability Policy Studies*, vol. 16, no. 1, Summer 2005, p. 59.

64. Timothy E. Quill, "Is Physician-Assisted Suicide Ever Acceptable? It's Justified in Rare Cases," *Family Practice News*, June 1, 2007, p. 11.

65. Quill, "Is Physician-Assisted Suicide Ever Acceptable?" p. 11.

66. Quoted in Katherine Seligman, "Hastening the End," *San Francisco Chronicle*, June 8, 2008.

List of Illustrations

Index